HUMAN CLONING

HUMAN CLONING
RELIGIOUS RESPONSES

Ronald Cole-Turner
editor

Westminster John Knox Press
Louisville, Kentucky

Book design by Jennifer K. Cox
Cover design by Dean Nicklas

First edition
Published by Westminster John Knox Press
Louisville, Kentucky

This book is printed on acid-free paper that meets the
American National Standards Institute Z39.48 standard. ∞

PRINTED IN THE UNITED STATES OF AMERICA
97 98 99 00 01 02 03 04 05 06 — 10 9 8 7 6 5 4 3 2 1

Library of Congress Cataloging-in-Publication Data

Human cloning : religious responses / Ronald Cole-Turner, editor. —
1st ed.
       p.   cm.
  Includes bibliographical references.
  ISBN 0-664-25771-2
  1. Cloning—Religious aspects—Christianity.   2. Cloning—Moral
and ethical aspects.   3. Human genetics—Religious aspects—
Christianity.   4. Human genetics—Moral and ethics.   I. Cole
Turner, Ronald, date.
QH442.2.H861997
241'.64957—DC21   97-30287

Contents

Contributors

DONALD BRUCE is the Director of the Society, Religion and Technology Project of the Church of Scotland.

TED PETERS is Professor of Systematic Theology at Pacific Lutheran Theological Seminary and the Graduate Theological Union.

ABIGAIL RIAN EVANS is Associate Professor of Practical Theology at Princeton Theological Seminary.

SIR JOHN POLKINGHORNE is former President of Queens' College, Cambridge, and a member of the Human Genetics Advisory Commission (U.K.).

PETER J. PARIS is the Elmer G. Homrighausen Professor of Social Ethics at Princeton Theological Seminary.

KAREN LEBACQZ is the Robert Gordon Sproul Professor of Theological Ethics at the Pacific School of Religion and the Graduate Theological Union.

STANLEY M. HAUERWAS is the Gilbert T. Rowe Professor of Theological Ethics at the Divinity School, Duke University.

JOEL SHUMAN is a Ph.D. Candidate at the Divinity School.

DAVID BYERS is Director, Committee on Science and Human Values, United States Catholic Conference, Washington, D.C.

BRENT WATERS is a D. Phil. Candidate in Moral Theology at Oxford University.

R. ALBERT MOHLER, JR., is President and Professor of Christian Theology at the Southern Baptist Theological Seminary, Louisville.

ROGER L. SHINN is the Reinhold Niebuhr Professor Emeritus of Social Ethics at Union Theological Seminary in New York.

RONALD COLE-TURNER is the H. Parker Sharp Associate Professor of Theology and Ethics at Pittsburgh Theological Seminary.

Acknowledgments

The "Motions on Cloning" and "Cloning Animals and Humans: A Supplementary Report," are reprinted by permission of the Principal Clerk of the Church of Scotland.

"Remarks in Response to News Reports on the Cloning of Mammals" is reprinted by permission of the Secretariat for Pro-Life Activities of the National Conference of Catholic Bishops.

The "Statement from the United Methodist Genetic Science Task Force" is reprinted by permission of the General Board for Church and Society of the United Methodist Church.

The "Resolution on Cloning" of the Trustees of the Christian Life Commission of the Southern Baptist Convention is reprinted by permission of the Commission.

The "Statement on Cloning" by the Genetics Committee of the United Church Board for Homeland Ministries of the United Church of Christ is © 1997 by the United Church Board for Homeland Ministries, Division of Education and Publication and reprinted by permission.

Preface

The announcement in February 1997 of the birth of Dolly the cloned sheep[1] triggered a sudden interest in theology. Everywhere, it seemed, people wondered if scientists were on the threshold of "playing God."

Are there any moral and theological limits to technology?

If we *can* clone a human being, *should* we?

Would such an act violate a God-given boundary? And if so, then what will happen to us if, at some moment in the not too distant future in an obscure laboratory somewhere, a few human beings cross this boundary? Will we all be the poorer? Will the image of God in us fade away altogether, precisely because we have preferred to create ourselves in our own image?

Or would we merely be living out our God-given destiny, using our brains and our hands to transform the earth, taming the roughness of nature and even of our own genes so that they conform more fully to what God intends and what morality requires?

A generation ago, when it first became imaginable that something like nuclear transfer cloning would be achieved in mammals and eventually in human beings, Paul Ramsey issued this classic warning: "Men ought not to play God before they learn to be men, and after they have learned to be men they will not play God."[2] Efforts to engineer our offspring, Ramsey argued, would defy the God-given limitation of our humanity. Better to live within our limits than destroy our humanity by transgressing them.

In response to Ramsey, Joseph Fletcher insisted that there is nothing more human than to assume responsibility, to use our technology, to exercise control where possible, and to bring human procreation under the guidance of ethical choice.

> The future is not to be sought in the stars but in us, in human beings. We don't pray for rain, we irrigate and seed clouds; we don't pray for cures, we rely on medicine. The excuses of ignorance and helplessness are growing thin. This is the direction of the biological revolution—that we turn more and more from creatures to creators.[3]

The authors in this volume stand for the most part closer to Ramsey than to Fletcher. Several state their opposition to cloning in unmistakable terms. Others try to find a place between the extremes of Ramsey and Fletcher, between an unequivocal "No" and an optimistic "Yes."

Shall we clone? Well, maybe. Their maybe is not equivocation or indecisiveness. It is an invitation to discussion. It is willingness to hear the reasons, theological and prudential, for and against, and to weigh them carefully.

All of the authors here agree in this: The possibility of human cloning raises profound theological and ethical concerns, and it is imperative that Christians respond in faith, even if they find themselves disagreeing with other Christians. There is something far worse than theological disagreement, and that is theological silence. We who write in these pages agree that Christians must not be silent in the public debate about cloning.

For our society to make its way blithely into the practice of human cloning without having heard the concerns of Christians would be a great failure on the part of the church. We offer these essays as a challenge to churches and Christians everywhere to join the dialogue that will determine the shape of the human future.

In June 1997, the National Bioethics Advisory Commission issued its report, *Cloning Human Beings*, in response to the request of President Clinton. In the Recommendations (see Appendix I, page 131), the Commission advises in favor of a provisional or temporary ban on any attempts to use cloning technology to produce a child. The primary reason for the ban is that any attempts now would be completely unsafe. But as technology advances, as it inevitably will, cloning to produce a child may become reasonably safe, perhaps even safer than the traditional means of conception. If so, will that mean there are no lasting objections to cloning? Will human cloning then be an acceptable way to produce a child?

If there are lasting objections to cloning, they will be religious. The Commission wisely recognizes the importance of religious perspectives and seeks to "encourage widespread and continuing deliberation on these issues in order to further our understanding of the ethical and social implication of this technology."[4]

Indeed, let us deliberate. Let us pray for wisdom. Let us debate. Let us yearn for guidance. Nothing less than the future of the human race is at stake.

Ronald Cole-Turner

NOTES

1. I. Wilmot et al., "Viable Offspring Derived from Fetal and Adult Mammalian Cells," *Nature* 385 (1997): 810–13.
2. Paul Ramsey, *Fabricated Man: The Ethics of Genetic Control* (New Haven, Conn.: Yale University Press, 1970), 138.
3. Joseph Fletcher, *The Ethics of Genetic Control: Ending Reproductive Roulette* (Garden City, N.Y.: Doubleday, 1974), 200.
4. The National Bioethics Advisory Commission, *Cloning Human Beings* (Rockville, Maryland: June 1997): 110; excerpts reprinted in Appendix I.

1

A View from Edinburgh

DONALD M. BRUCE

WHEN I ASKED DR. Ian Wilmut three years ago to take part in a working group on the ethics of nonhuman genetic engineering for the Church of Scotland,[1] I had no notion that the Edinburgh mammalian embryologist would one day become a world-famous name. When Ian told me about the nuclear transfer work at the nearby Roslin Institute which would lead to the first two cloned sheep, Megan and Morag,[2] it was clear he was talking about an important technical breakthrough. But we never foresaw the scale of the reaction when Dolly was announced a year later. In our different ways we all found ourselves part of one of those rare moments in science and technology which, rightly or wrongly, captures the imagination of the whole world. The event became as much a media circus as a piece of science and an ethical challenge. It remains to be seen whether the science or the circus will have the greater long-term impact. This problem is interesting since it concerns not only ethics of a science so new that its ink is still wet on the page, but also public perceptions in the age of the Internet.

Technology and Imagination

To use technology is to do something God-given. It is inherent in our nature that human beings find ways to shape the created order around us. When Genesis speaks of the image of God, something above and beyond mere creatureliness is implied. Men and women bear something creative in our very being. The curiosity and inventiveness in the picture of Adam naming the animals is familiar enough to us all. It is not just that we want to classify. We imagine beyond mere description, and in imagining conceive new things—things that have not been before. Technology is the rather odd word we use for what extends beyond knowledge and sees application also. It enables us not only to call a particular woolly mammal "sheep" but to see what sheep could mean to humankind.

It is a very long step from saying "sheep" to imagining the asexual genetic replication of human beings. Yet that is where we are. One of the most striking reactions to the work of Dr. Wilmut and his colleagues at Roslin is the way in which the world's media did an instant quantum leap. From an unexpected discovery in mammalian biology—reprogramming the somatic cells of an adult mammal and so creating an entire new animal asexually—the focus jumped straight to imagining a world peopled with human clones. In the orgy of speculation in which the media indulged, comparatively few paused and asked what it already means for our relationships with the animal kingdom, which may well remain the largest issue regarding cloning. It is perhaps a reflection of our preoccupation with ourselves to which this chapter is, in part, a response.

I also want to address a question which seems to underlie much of the general concern: "How on earth did we get here?" Many are wondering how our God-given abilities have apparently brought us to the verge of photocopying ourselves—without our even noticing it. This has added force to a growing undercurrent of concern across Western Europe about how few people have any say about the way in which biotechnology is being allowed to develop. Have we allowed the imaginations of those to whom society entrusts this particular expression of the image of God to become too free, set loose from their ethical and social moorings?

"If I were going to Dublin, I wouldn't start from here. . ." So runs the apocryphal response made to the traveller lost in the heart of rural Ireland. It was not with cloning humans in mind that Roslin began its series of embryological experiments. The purpose was to find better ways to produce genetically modified sheep. In 1986, Roslin researchers made the ground-breaking discovery that it was possible to produce therapeutic proteins in the milk of sheep and other mammals by introducing one or two genes of human origin into the animal.[3] This has since been developed by the Edinburgh company, PPL Therapeutics, into a world-class example of animal genetic engineering. Today there is, with relatively little impact on the animal, a wide range of potential medical products in prospect. The leading protein made in this way is alpha-1anti-trypsin, which can help counteract the lung damage found in emphysema and cystic fibrosis.[4] It successfully completed its first stage of clinical trials in mid-1997.

⚹ Genetic engineering in sheep, performed by injecting into an early embryo, is a very hit-and-miss process, with about a 1% success rate.[5] Roslin's aim is to do the modification in a cell culture, select the right one, and then "grow" a full animal from the cells. This is possible with the embryonic stem cells of mice, but not in larger animals. Roslin's recent success in nuclear transfer cloning, with an unmodified sheep, was an attempt to find a way around this problem. Their next step is to try the same thing with cells from a genetically modified sheep, to produce a sheep which has the relevant gene in exactly the right place. If it works, it would enable a more precise manipulation using fewer animals, and would also open the door to a much wider range of genetic changes and applications.

In many ways, therefore, cloning was a side issue. From the point of view of animal genetics and embryology, Dolly was the result of a natural progression of ideas, each step seen as a logical progression from the previous one. This is the phenomenon sometimes known as "gradualism." It is notoriously difficult to realize the full ethical import of the complete series of steps, until suddenly one of them produces something as tangible as a live sheep cloned from an udder cell, and we wake up abruptly to something that has been happening imperceptibly.

Accusations of secrecy were unfounded. Roslin and PPL had every reason to publish at the earliest possible moment and were not unusually secretive. They observed the normal restrictions on disclosure before publication in the scientific literature as required when filing a European patent.[6] Much the same question had already been asked a year before, when Megan and Morag were cloned from an embryo cell line. That we had largely forgotten this, certainly here in Scotland, was in part because the Dunblane massacre overwhelmed our senses a mere week later. This is itself a reflection of the power of the media to tell us what to focus on for the present, and of our finite human attention span in an increasingly information-saturated world.

Prospects and Problems for Cloning Animals

If cloning by nuclear transfer began as a by-product of a broader research program, its developers have not been slow to recognize its commercial and scientific potential as a deliberate tool for agricultural production and research.[7] Cloning has been practiced only to a very limited extent, mostly in cattle, by splitting embryos, itself not without ethical and welfare concerns. PPL Therapeutics might clone 5–10 animals from one single genetically modified cell line. Thereafter, these animals would be bred naturally, as "founders" of a set of lines of genetically modified animals from whose milk they would extract and purify the relevant protein. There would be no advantage in cloning beyond this first point.[8] Such medical applications tend to be on a small scale.

Several potential applications in conventional meat or milk production present a very different picture. In commercial animal breeding, the selected animals at the top of the breeding pyramid have highly desirable characteristics and are thus very valuable. Cloning these animals could give farmers the prospect of raising the breeding value of their herds, shortcutting the lengthy timescales and practical hurdles of conventional breeding. If there were a clear benefit to the farmer to start off with prime stock, to produce the best beef or pork, this might seem to have its attractions. Alternatively, the cloned animals could be sold as they are to farmers who simply feed up the animals for slaughter. Again, the breeder might want to clone a series of promising animals in a breeding program in order to test how the same "genotype" responded to different environmental changes.

Such breeding applications would be more relevant to cattle and pigs, which are of higher value than sheep. As of today, this is all speculation on the very inadequate basis of one empirical result in one breed of sheep, obtained after many failures. The underlying science is as yet little understood. Whatever the commercial or academic pressures, it might be irresponsible to proceed too quickly without establishing a more basic understanding of the mechanisms involved, which inevitably takes time. For the moment, a number of problems could mean the technology does not develop very far. Large fetuses have sometimes resulted from cloning, for reasons which are not understood, and there could be adverse effects on fertility or aging processes. Different farm animal species also differ quite markedly in embryology. There are indications that cloning might well work in cattle but could be very difficult in pigs.

These problems have been largely overlooked in discussions of human cloning. That quantum leap from sheep to human beings may be less certain than some have predicted. For example, from what is currently known, there could be a considerable risk to a mother bearing a cloned fetus, which could rule any experiment out on medical grounds. Naive views about the unbounded power of science to overcome all hurdles are surprisingly prevalent among both the champions who promote a new technology and those who fear it.

Another important practical concern is how far genetic diversity can be reduced without adverse effects. Cloning would only be prudent if it did not threaten this diversity. Fields upon fields of genetically identical cattle are unlikely. The more the genetic "pool" is narrowed to a limited number of lines of animals, the greater the risk of concentrating detrimental traits alongside the desired ones or of being vulnerable to having all the breeding lines wiped out by disease. Embryo freezing and gene banks might offset this, but having to resort to such a technical fix begs the question whether it was the wrong avenue in the first place.

Is Animal Cloning a Step Too Far?

Beneath the pragmatics, however, lie deeper ethical concerns. There is nothing in what is commonly described as the scientific method to say on what grounds we should hold back from what could be done in technology. This is perhaps because of too narrow a view of the scientific method, a view which sees it as an independent entity, rather than a value-laden activity answerable to both God and to human society. From a Christian standpoint, our shaping of God's creation is constrained by more than the limits of technology.

Over recent years we have seen important progress in molecular biology and related disciplines. This has given us much better understanding of the mechanisms which control many of the processes of life. On the other hand, the more powerful the methods we use, the more we need to consider not only what is possible for humanity, but what is happening to us as people if we say "yes" to every possibility which science may make possible. Such an unfettered view of human progress and improvement is not consonant with a gospel in which human finiteness and fallibility form the context for a critique of the human project. To be answerable to God for the way we use our many talents has two important implications. One is in the sphere of human relationships, and the other arises from God's ordinance to us to care for the rest of creation. On both these counts, not all technical progress in biotechnology is necessarily desirable. A sense of restraint may be needed.

On what grounds might such restraint be demanded? Looking first at animal cloning, we recognize that one of the most characteristic features of God's creation is its variety. Throughout the Bible, in commandments and stories and poetry, the overall picture is of a rich and wonderful creation, whose sheer diversity is a cause of praise to its creator. It could be argued that to produce a replica on demand would be to go against something basic and God-given about the nature of life. While it is true that cloning is common enough in plants, this is not the case in mammals, where God has ordained sexual reproduction to be the norm. Where God sets up a system of diversification, it is a testimony to human nature that we use our imagination to make replicas of what we think is the best. Where God opens up boundless possibilities for the whole life of an animal, humans would reduce them to a narrow blueprint, for their functional value.

The fact that the dynamics of selective breeding have to be balanced by the need to maintain genetic diversity reflects something of the nature of things. At the least, it might suggest that cloning would be absolutely wrong, no matter what it was being used for. This intuition runs deep in many people I have spoken to over the past months, both inside and outside the church.

There are also questions of scale and intention, however. Strictly speaking, producing a cloned animal is a by-product of Roslin's nuclear transfer method, not the main intention. In this context, it seems hard to rule it out ethically. Of all the applications of genetic engineering, therapeutic proteins in sheep's milk is one of the least ethically problematical, unless one holds to an inherent objection to all genetic engineering. A detailed analysis is given elsewhere,[9] but in summary there are obvious human benefits with few animal problems. In general, welfare concerns seem to be minimal once past the experimental stage, and the dignity and nature of the animal is not violated by producing in its milk a protein related to one she already produces. To extend the potential of this by nuclear transfer, where the intent is not to clone as such, would not seem to raise insuperable objections, since it is the instrumental aspect of cloning that raises the deepest concern. Moreover, if an absolute ethical prohibition were made of animal cloning, it would have to reckon with precluding certain of the medical and animal benefits which PPL Therapeutics' pharmaceutical applications may enable. On the other hand, this does not give carte blanche for all animal genetic manipulations. Animal welfare issues may rule out some options, and each type of use would need careful ethical assessment, but those are questions we already face.

Animal cloning might therefore be acceptable in the limited context of research or specialist transgenic applications, where natural methods would not work, and where the main intention was not the clone as such but producing an animal of a known genetic composition. In contrast, the Church of Scotland has declared as unacceptable its use in routine animal production, where natural methods exist but have been side-stepped on the grounds of economics or convenience. "This would represent one step too far beyond conventional selective breeding in the way we use animals as commodities. The approach that, whatever use we find for animals, we could clone them to do it more efficiently brings the mass production principles of the factory too far into the animal kingdom. Just as in the Old Testament an ox was not to be muzzled while treading out the grain, animals have certain freedoms which we should preserve. We may use animals to an extent, but we need to remind ourselves that they are firstly God's creatures, to whom we may not do everything we like."

Another factor is the pressure of consumerism. If the root motive to clone meat-producing animals is ultimately to benefit the supermarket production system, in consequential terms this suggests a poor justification for a questionable intervention. To manipulate animals to be born, grow and reach maturity for sale and slaughter at exactly the time we want them, to suit production schedules, suggests treating an animal too much as if it were just a widget.

Human Cloning

The imagination of Dolly's creators stopped firmly short of the line of cloning human beings. From the outset Dr. Wilmut and his colleagues have made their ethical opposition to this idea quite unequivocal. As far as can be judged, most in the United Kingdom would agree. An outright deontological ethical prohibition appears to be almost a matter of instinct to people of all kinds of moral outlooks on the world. Willfully to copy the human genetic identity seems to go beyond something inherent in human dignity and individuality.

A human is unique, and cloning would be seen as compromising the uniqueness that God has given to that one person. When looked at more closely, what is actually compromised turns out to be more subtle.

It was quickly pointed out that it is a very reductionist view of human beings to identify human individuality solely with genetic identity. Moreover, what we call "identical twins" are in fact more similar to each other than Dolly is to her precursor (whose name, interestingly, has never been discussed). Firstly, the nuclear transfer technique has combined the cell nucleus of one sheep with the cytoplasm from another. This cytoplasm includes the mitochondria, which have their own DNA. Already one area of interest is the effect the different mitochondria in the cytoplasm—which among other things affect the process of aging—might possibly have on Dolly, compared with her precursor, who has different mitochondrial DNA. Secondly, and arguably more important in terms of individuality, the environment in which a nuclear transfer clone would grow, both in the womb and outside, would be quite different. Such logic has led a few to challenge the predominant reaction against human cloning and ask "Why not?"

The cases advanced in favor of cloning human beings seem often to have overlooked and confused several things. One is that the application of Roslin's nuclear transfer methods is limited to medical applications that stop well short of cloning a full human being. Another is associated with somewhat bizarre notions of human potential improvement, often mistaking cloning for human germ-line genetic enhancement. A third area is ideological, and certain cults that focus on extraterrestrial interventions see cloning as a step forward in human spiritual development, without specifying too clearly what genetic replication would achieve that normal reproduction fails to do.

Against these notions, there is a basic principle that to replicate any human being technologically is a fundamentally instrumental act towards two unique individuals—the one from whom the clone is taken, and the other the clone itself. This is not the same as twinning. There is a world of difference ethically between choosing to clone from a known existing individual and the unpredictable occurrence of twins of unknown nature in the womb. The nature of cloning is that the clone is created for the primary benefit not of the individual but of some third party, as means to an end. This represents unacceptable human abuse and such a potential for exploitation that it should be outlawed worldwide in the form of an international treaty by which it would be classed as a crime against humanity.

Short of cloning to produce a human being, there are other human research applications that might be made of Roslin's

techniques. Lord Winston listed some possibilities, all of which
are speculative and some of which would require some significant breakthroughs to achieve.[10]

Many of these would raise serious ethical problems, such as the
deliberate creation of cloned embryos for research. This seems
too close to the slippery slope of human cloning to be counte-
nanced, quite apart from the ongoing controversies about embryo
research. Less contentious might be to take a tissue sample, develop a cell line, reprogram the cells using Roslin's technique so
that they create a different whole organ, which could be used for
transplant purposes. No one knows if this is possible, nor whether
the same slippery slope would exist. Such possible developments
would require more careful ethical consideration, once it became
apparent what was actually envisaged, with widespread public
consultation.

Controls—Can We Go Back?

This raises a last question about the control of such research. At
the beginning of this chapter I asked if we have allowed scientists
too much free rein, to the point where they are indulging rather
than serving society, and abusing their God-given talents. International treaties would not prevent the unscrupulous from abusing
these techniques, but the fear of public discovery and the risk of
criminal proceedings against all involved might deter some who
would otherwise proceed. A second level of defense against misuse would be an ethical charter for scientists, by which a declaration not to engage in such activities was recognized as a standard
for membership by professional bodies. The concept of the ethical
scientist whose work is open to public scrutiny remains the best an-
tidote of all to the misuse of our inventive capacities.

Alongside this there needs to be a greater sense of public accountability by researchers in order to give the public a reasonable
chance either to support or reject the more significant emerging
areas of biotechnology. In many spheres of research, there is an
accountability deficit in the existing procedures whereby research
priorities are set. There are signs of frustration at this, especially

in Europe. Inappropriate areas such as patenting have become the arenas for ethical debate, because there are few other official channels to which the ordinary citizen has effective access. Committees of "the great and the good" are often too dominated by industry perspectives to enable a fair hearing for objectors. The setting up of a standing transgenic animal ethics commission in the Netherlands, whose interim decisions are open to public debate as an intrinsic part of the evaluation, seems to offer some pointers to the way ahead. There are no easy solutions to this problem, but failure to pay attention could result in an alienated citizenship. If God means us to do genetics and embryology, then God has also provided us with civil society to help us keep the human imagination in the bounds of God's kingdom.

NOTES

1. "Engineering Genesis," Science, Religion and Technology Project Report, Church of Scotland, in preparation.
2. K.H.S. Campbell et al., "Sheep Cloned by Nuclear Transfer from a Cultured Cell Line," *Nature* 380 (1996): 64–66.
3. G. Wright et al., "High Level Expression of Active Human alpha-1antitrypsin in the Milk of Transgenic Sheep," *Biotechnology* 9 (1991): 830–34.
4. Ibid.
5. I.Wilmut, "Modification of Farm Animals by Genetic Engineering and Immunomodulation," in *Issues in Agricultural Bioethics*, ed. T.B. Mepham, G.A. Tucker, and J. Wiseman (Nottingham: Nottingham University Press, 1995).
6. In contrast to the United States, in the European patent system any prior disclosure nullifies the claim.
7. J. Williams, article submitted for publication to *Farmers Weekly*, 1997.
8. R. James, personal communication, 1997.
9. "Engineering Genesis."
10. R. M. Winston, "The Promise of Cloning for Human Medicine," *BMA Journal* 314 (1997): 7085.

2

Cloning Shock

A Theological Reaction

TED PETERS

■■■ SCIENCE SHOCKS. ■■■■■■■■■■■■■■■
Religion reacts.

The moment cloning was announced, immediately and intuitively the world recognized that this is a theological issue. It's
more than just science. It's more than just a new technological
discovery. It's more than just an occasion for jokes about the
name "Dolly" or, as found in the announcement appearing with
the picture of two sheep on the cover of *Time*, "Will There Ever
Be Another You?" (read "ewe"). This science raises religious
questions, and the ambient anxiety raises ethical ire.

Within hours of the release of news regarding Ian Wilmut's
cloning achievement of producing a live adult lamb from cells
originating from a sheep mammary gland, the Church of Scotland
released its theological analysis. The *Time* magazine coverage
spoke of "soulquakes" and asked theological questions of readers:
"Can souls be xeroxed?"[1] The March 3, 1997 cover of *Der
Spiegel* pictured multiple copies of Adolph Hitler, Albert Ein-
stein, and Claudia Schiffers, along with a caption in large capital
letters, "Der Sundenfall" (the fall into sin).

Radio, TV, and print reporters interviewed theologians and
ethicists of many religious persuasions. The press was looking for
ethical outrage, looking for someone to declare a desecration of
something sacred or to shriek fear that human individuals would lose
their individuality. A *Time* magazine poll asked, "Is it against God's
will to clone human beings?" 74% answered yes; 19% answered
no.[2] "Stop Cloning Around" was the title of a *Christianity Today* editorial; and a *Christian Century* editorial said that "cloning a person
would violate that person's freedom to establish her own identity."[3] Such outrage could also be found by President Bill Clinton's

National Bioethics Advisory Commission as it interviewed theological ethicists such as Gilbert Meilaender and Lisa Sowle Cahill. Martin Marty assessed the situation by observing, "Crossing the new scientific horizon produces intuitions that science now possesses the key to a door most would rather have locked forever. The folk language draws on cliches: 'Don't fool with Mother Nature' and 'You shouldn't play God.' " [4]

Not every theologian or ethicist was outraged, to be sure. Philip Hefner at the Chicago Center for Religion and Science (CCRS) told the press that we should be stewards of this new cloning capability and that we are accountable to God for what we do.[5] The Center for Theology and the Natural Sciences (CTNS) at the Graduate Theological Union in Berkeley told the press that cloning is potentially good, because "God could be seen as continuing to create through human agency." CTNS went on to caution us: If cloning becomes used in human reproduction, we as a society need to guard the dignity of children against possible commodification and merchandising. Whether in a mood of outrage or a mood of cautionary stewardship, the secular media and the theological community immediately agreed that human cloning is a religious issue.

In what follows I plan to look at the scientific shock — that is, look briefly at just what was accomplished by the cloning experiment at Roslin. From the scientific point of view the breakthrough consists in showing that we can begin with an already differentiated adult cell and return it to the predifferentiated state to initiate normal development in a cloned mammal.

Next I will turn to the religious and ethical reaction, giving particular attention to the fear that somehow human individuality and identity might be threatened as we think about cloning human beings. Against what appears to be the emerging widespread presumption, I will argue on scientific and theological grounds that we can safely say that no serious threat to human individuality or identity exists here.

I will then proceed to assert that on distinctively theological grounds no good reason for proscribing human cloning can be mustered. However, this does not preclude other grounds for caution. I will caution us to guard against misuse of cloning as a "for sale" service in human reproduction on the grounds that it risks commodifying children—that is, cloning along with some other reproductive high-tech services could risk treating children with quality-control standards that might reduce them to merchandise. I would argue that theologically and culturally this is a moment in time when we need to be ethically alert and take steps to protect the dignity of future children.

What Was the Science at Roslin?

Along with colleagues at the Roslin Institute in Edinburgh, Scotland, embryologist Ian Wilmut devised a cloning procedure, patented it, announced it to the press February 22, 1997, and then published the details in the February 27, 1997 issue of *Nature*. The Roslin team removed cells from the udder of a pregnant Finn Dorset ewe, placed them in a culture, and starved them of nutrients for a week until the cells became quiescent—that is, they arrested the normal cycle of cell division, initiating a state akin to hibernation. Second, they took an unfertilized egg, or oocyte, from a Scottish Blackface ewe and removed the nucleus. When removing the nucleus with the DNA, they left the remaining cytoplasm intact. Third, the scientists placed the quiescent cell next to the oocyte, and then they introduced pulses of electric current. The gentle electric shock caused the cells to fuse, and the oocyte cytoplasm accepted the quiescent DNA. A second electric pulse initiated normal cell division. Fourth, after six days of cell division, the merged embryo was implanted into the uterus of another Blackface ewe and brought through pregnancy to birth. The newborn lamb was named Dolly.

A key question has apparently been answered with this experiment: Is cell differentiation reversible? The answer seems to be yes. Embryonic cells are predifferentiated. Adult cells are normally differentiated in order to perform the particular tasks of particular parts of the body. For example, genes for hair are turned on in the hair while genes for toenails are turned off in hair but on where the toenails belong. In theory, cloning could be accomplished by employing cells in their predifferentiated state. The trick here was to make an adult differentiated cell function as an undifferentiated embryonic cell. According to Phil Heffner, "The fact that a lamb was derived from an adult cell confirms that differentiation of that cell did not involve the irreversible modification of genetic material required for development to term."[6]

In 1993 at the George Washington Medical Center in Washington, D.C., Robert J. Stillman and Jerry Hall cloned seventeen human embryos. These clones were made by splitting other pre-embryos after a few cell divisions but prior to cell differentiation. The embryos were allowed to develop for six days. Because the pre-embryos selected for the experiment contained identifiable genetic defects, they were not expected to survive pregnancy. They didn't. Similarly, shortly after the Roslin story broke, Don Wolf at the Oregon Regional Primate Research Center reported cloning monkeys—that is, making twins from embryos. The significant advance of the Roslin team over the Washington and Oregon experiments is that Dolly's DNA was taken from an already differentiated adult cell and, in the host oocyte, began division again at the predifferentiated stage. The scientific breakthrough is that we know now that future cloning could begin with the cells of adult animals, perhaps even human beings.

The procedure was not clean and easy. The successful cloning of Dolly was accompanied by numerous misfires. Out of 277 tries, the Roslin scientists were able to make only 29 embryos survive beyond six days. At fourteen days 62% of the fetuses in ewe wombs were lost, a significantly greater proportion than the estimate of 6% after natural mating. Eight ewes gave birth to five lambs, with all but one dying shortly thereafter. Dolly is the only one to survive. Triumph is accompanied by loss.

Should We Clone Human Beings?

Many issues of an ethical if not aesthetic or religious character leap to our attention, such as whether we should clone animals on a mass scale. Would cloning technology applied to the most marketable cows in order to enhance meat production further commodify animals and deny them any respect beyond mere instrumental value for human consumption? Would cloning, like other genetic manipulations of research animals in order to make them into medicine factories, be further evidence of human speciesism and tyrannous dominion over the natural world?

The overriding ethical issue is this: Should we clone human beings? This question sends an electrical charge into our religious sensibilities. It shocks us into theological reflection. It may not be immediately clear what we ought to think, but we know we need to think something. When receiving a shock from an electrical outlet, we immediately withdraw our hand to safety. So also, it seems, cloning shock causes us to withdraw immediately into what we hope will be safety, namely, religious conservatism. We say, "No." And we add, "We say no because God says no." But, I ask: Does God really say "No"?

Back in 1971 James Watson predicted this debate. Watson, along with Francis Crick, won the Nobel Prize for the discovery of the double helix structure of DNA. Writing on cloning for the *Atlantic Monthly,* he said "The first reaction of most people to the arrival of these asexually produced children, I suspect, would be one of despair." He then went on to suggest that people with strong religious backgrounds would want to "de-emphasize all those forms of research which would circumvent the normal sexual reproductive process."[7] He seems to have been correct, or at least partially correct.

In February 1997 the Society, Religion and Technology Project of the Church of Scotland said that cloning human beings would be "ethically unacceptable as a matter of principle." According to Christian belief, cloning would be a "violation of the uniqueness of human life, which God has given to each of us and to no one else."[8] This argument that each individual person has a unique identity that would be violated by cloning has been repeated frequently in religious and secular circles.

Let us examine this argument more closely. The first assumption here seems to be that, in order for a human person to have an individual identity, he or she must have a unique genome. The second assumption seems to be that God has ordained that each person have a genome that differs from every other person. The third assumption seems to be that through this genetic technology human beings could accidentally produce two persons with the same identity and, thereby, violate the divine creator's intention. On the basis of these scientific and theological assumptions, the ethical conclusion drawn here is this: no cloning.

The first assumption is empirically false. What distinguishes a clone is that he or she would have the same genome as the person from whom the DNA was originally taken. Both the original DNA donor and the clone would have identical genotypes. But, we might ask, does this mean they would have identical phenotypes? No, because DNA does not express itself in lock-step fashion. There are variations in expression and spontaneous mutations. In addition, environmental factors are frequently decisive. Food and exercise and health care and countless other environmental factors influence gene activity. If the DNA donor and clone are reared a generation apart, let alone in separate locations, similarities will be noticeable, to be sure, but differences will abound.

In addition, we have the experience of twins. Like clones, identical twins are born with identical genomes. Despite parents who may occasionally dress them alike and treat them alike, they grow up as separate and distinct individuals. Each has his or her own interior consciousness, sense of self, thought processes, and ethical responsibility. Even if studies in behavioral genetics eventually show strong DNA influence on predispositions to certain forms of behavior, or even an uncanny affinity for one another, they remain two separate individuals with separate lives to lead. A clone would be a delayed twin, and, due to the delay, would probably experience even more independence than two born at the same time.

No reputable theological position has ever held that two twins share a single soul. Each has his or her own soul, his or her own connection to God. The human soul, theologically speaking, is not formed from DNA as the phenotype is formed from the genotype. The soul is not a metaphysical appendage to the physical. To the question asked by *Time* magazine, "Can souls be xeroxed?", we might answer, "No." Or, perhaps, we might answer, "If yes, then the result is two souls, not one."

The key to understanding the soul theologically is not its emergence beyond the physical as psyche or mind. Rather, the key is understanding the soul in terms of our relationship to God. The unique relation of a person to God is not determined by DNA. It is determined by God's active grace, by God's desire to love us as we are.

Karen Lebacqz, developing the concept of soul in the work of Helmut Thielicke and applying it to the cloning issue, contends that the soul is not an attribute of our own but rather constitutes an "alien dignity." Neither our individuality nor our soul are threatened by cloning: "My value or dignity is given by God; it derives from the fact that God loves me," Lebacqz writes. "In such an understanding, 'soul' is not an individual possession but a statement about relationship. Soul has to do with our standing before God."[9]

No sound theological argument against cloning could be raised on the grounds that it violates an alleged God-given identity. Our identities in society come from growing up in society. Our identities before God come from God's ongoing grace and from our desire or lack of desire to live in close communion with God.

Should We Ban Human Cloning?

At a press conference in the Oval Office at the White House on March 4, 1997, President Clinton described cloning as more than mere science: "It is a matter of morality and spirituality as well." He added: "Each human life is unique, born of a miracle that reaches beyond laboratory science. I believe we must respect this profound gift and resist the temptation to replicate ourselves." With this introduction he proceeded to issue a directive that "bans the use of any federal funds for any cloning of human beings" and asked the scientific community in the private sector for a "voluntary moratorium on the cloning of human beings." He then asked the National Bioethics Advisory Commission to study the matter and come up with policy recommendations.

During the question-and-answer period he described people

who might want to replicate themselves as "trying to play God." Politics, like science, can evoke religion.

Washington is not the only capital in which the proposal to ban human cloning has been discussed. The Select Committee on Genetics and Public Policy of the California Senate held hearings on April 9, 1997. On behalf of the American Society for Reproductive Medicine, Ryszard J. Chetowski, M.D., testified that "the practice of cloning an existing human being by nuclear transfer—that is, replicating an existing or previously existing person by transferring the nucleus of an adult, differentiated cell into an oocyte in which the nucleus has been removed (an enucleated egg)—is unacceptable."[10] He continued by distinguishing between the use of cloning to produce a human being and the use of the same technique to produce beneficial medical therapies. Chetowski supports embryo research that will likely lead to improving the success of bone marrow transplants, repairing spinal cord injuries, and replacing the skin of burn victims. A ban on cloning human beings should leave embryo research intact, Chetowski believes.

Francis C. J. Pizzulli offered to the California Senate what he thought was an avowedly secular and nonreligious argument for a ban on cloning, namely, that each human being has the right to a unique genome. What he considered "valid secular state interests" are found "in the protection of individuality, autonomy, and privacy. . . protecting a citizen's right to a uniquely undetermined genotype."[11] The concept of human right is here applied to the uniqueness of genotype, and he is asking for a policy to protect that right by prohibiting the design or determination of a genotype in advance by cloning.

This proposed protection of strictly unique genotypes raises a logical question: Would twins be in violation of each other's right to a unique genotype? If a set of twins were judged to be in such violation, which one would go to jail? Or would both go to jail? Although Pizzulli himself was less than fully clear on this, others who hold this view typically argue that twins are naturally determined whereas clones are determined by choice. Whereas nature dictates shared genomes in the case of twins, clones would be the result of intentional human decision. The argument, finally, is an argument against human choice in determining genotype. In short, this argument against human cloning represents the kind of conservative despair forecast by Watson for the religious communities, only here it is proposed as a secular rights' argument.

To repeat, individual identity is not at stake when cloning is the mode of a person's conception. And, even if it were, the assumption that each of us has a right to genotypical uniqueness would require some supporting evidence. The burden of proof would fall on the shoulders of the one making the assertion. I for one cannot anticipate a convincing argument. Along the way such an argument would have to take into account a potential threat toward the rights of twins. If twins should be seen as living in violation of genotypical uniqueness, it could lead to a public policy of pregnancy reduction or even infanticide to eliminate twins in the future.

An argument with this implication is overkill, much more than is necessary, simply to ban human cloning. This kind of argument betrays a veiled naturalism, a variant on the alleged "thou shalt not play God" commandment. It seems to presuppose that what nature bequeaths us prior to human choice has a higher moral status than what happens when we influence nature through technological intervention. It seems to presuppose that, because most people by nature have unique genomes, it ought to be that way. Twins are seen here as exceptions to natural law and to moral law. Twins may be excused, because they couldn't help it. Cloners may not be excused, because they could. The fact that clones are predetermined by human decision making is allegedly what makes cloning immoral and warrants legislation to ban the practice. What nature does is legal, and what we do will be moral if we copy nature. The argument commits the naturalistic fallacy: It tries to base an "ought" on an "is." It argues that, because nature has behaved in a certain way in the past, we ought to behave the same way in the future. This is a fallacy because moral judgments are intended to pull us forward toward a reality better than the one we have inherited. The situation as it is does not necessarily describe how it ought to be.

The idea of a ban on human cloning may be a good idea, even if supported to date by bad arguments. What other kinds of arguments should be brought to bear on the discussion leading toward public policy formulation? Specifically, what theological concerns are relevant to understanding the ethical implications of human cloning? My chief concern—and I grant that a long list of other concerns could rightly be introduced here—is the risk cloning might pose to the dignity of children. My concern for dignity is not based on a perceived threat to the individuality or identity of the child. Rather, it is based on the potential for cloning, along with other genetic technologies, to play into the hands of economic forces that will tend to commodify children. Whether this threat is sufficient to warrant an outright ban, I am unable to judge with certainty. Yet I wish to raise the warning in such a way that it contributes to the public discussion.

Dignity for Children: A Relational Treasure

As a theologian reading the New Testament, I interpret 1 John 4:19, "We love because [God] first loved us," with the following maxim: God loves each of us regardless of our genetic makeup, and we should do likewise. This religious commitment has a secular companion principle, namely, that we should treat each person as an end and not merely as a means for something more valuable. This is what I mean by dignity.[12]

Significant here is that dignity is a relational concept. Earlier I said that the soul should be understood theologically as referring to our relationship to God. Similarly, dignity is relational, even though we might not ordinarily think so. Ordinarily, we think of dignity as something inborn, something innate, an endowment by nature or by God that we as a body politic must revere in morality and law. That it is, at least philosophically speaking. Yet dignity as we actually experience it is relational. It is the experience of being treated as worthy and then incorporating into ourselves the sense of self-worth. When other people or when the law treats us individually as an end and not merely as a means to some further end, we gain a sense of our own fundamental value as a human being. Our ethical task is to impute dignity to those who may not already experience it, so that they might rise up and claim dignity for themselves. To treat a person as a person of worth is to love, and love is a relational force that enhances an individual's sense of self-worth.

It is not individuality or identity per se that constitutes a person's dignity. Uniqueness does not determine dignity. Our value as a person comes experientially from the people who love us and, ultimately if not ontologically, from God's love for us.

Certainly I am not alone in sensing that human cloning could pose a risk to the dignity of future children. But just what is the nature of that risk? Under which bridge do we locate the troll who might come up and snatch dignity away? Just where is the cloning shock going to hurt us?

Some theological ethicists fear that cloning, along with the advance of reproductive choice, will undermine the procreative unity of the family, and that this in turn will harm children. I disagree. I do not think that the problem of cloning lies in its impact on the sex life of mothers and fathers in families. The risk to children is not found in the replacement of sexual with asexual conception. Rather, it is found in thinking of children as products, as the outcome of technological reproduction with quality-control standards.

Cloning as a method of conception could in the medium-range future join with artificial insemination, donor semen and donor eggs, in vitro fertilization, and surrogate motherhood in expanding the range of choice in procreation. We can forecast that reproductive clinics would market cloning along with these other services to prospective parents. Although advertising typically cloaks the reproductive business in medical and health-care language, genetic and related technologies are finding a market with buyers.

We all know of infertile couples who strive and struggle to create a warm family, and we know that when a new baby comes into their world it is given love and devotion. How joyful they are when infertility therapy is successful. The fulfillment of the deep need many of us feel to create a family becomes translated into authentic love for children. Self-fulfillment for parents and dignity for children are not necessarily competitors; they can be complementary.

The new element with cloning and related genetic advances is quality control. The motives for a cloned conception are likely to include the desire to replicate a favorite relative or perhaps borrow DNA from someone known for good health or intelligence or physical strength. Genetic advances in general and cloning procedures in particular will increase the prospects of designer babies. Reproduction will come to look more and more like production. Babies will come to look more and more like products.

We can imagine the megalomaniac who might want to clone himself or herself. Such a person, out of pride, perhaps, might seek a form of immortality through children, akin to the motives of wealthy benefactors who have buildings named after themselves. The risk that such a child's dignity would be jeopardized is found in the prospect that role expectations might be so strong as to snuff out individual initiative. Christians like to think of our dignity as deriving in part from our being created in the image of God, the *imago dei*. The cloned child of a megalomaniac would bear, in addition to the *imago dei*, a superimposed image of the cloner, the *imago mei*. We intuitively want to avoid putting a child in such a position. Yet it is a likely scenario when cloning services go on sale.

What is more likely is the following. We can imagine a future couple sitting in the reception room of a reproductive clinic looking at an album. This album would contain pages of pictures of children with special DNA formulas, clones whose genotypes this clinic has paid royalties for and is licensed to sell. The parents-to-be begin with choice, begin with choosing the DNA profile of their future child. No doubt they will use quality criteria. If the technology fails—as technology frequently does—will they abort? If the baby is born and fails to meet expectations, will it be sent back to the factory? Will the parents ask for a refund? a discount? To what extent will such children be treated as commodities?

Is this risk sufficient to warrant a total ban on human cloning? Perhaps not. But warning sirens should sound to alert us of potential harm to the dignity of cloned children. Ethical thinking leading to public policy should be the order of the day.

I welcome the new world of expanded choice. I do not believe the way forward is to return to a time prior to choice, to curtail scientific development so that people will be permitted to procreate children only in the old-fashioned way. I do not believe the way forward is through denying choice. We cannot allow our ethics to derive from our fears of scientific advance. Rather, we need to construct ethical visions that take expanded choice into consideration. We need to construct visions of just what it means to treat children with dignity when they are the product—that is, when they are the gift—of advanced reproductive technology. For cloned children as well as children born the old-fashioned way, we need to be reminded that God loves each of us regardless of our genetic makeup. And we should do likewise.

NOTES

1. Jeffrey Kluger, "Will We Follow the Sheep?" *Time*, March 10, 1997, 67–73.
2. Ibid., p. 71.
3. Allen Verhey, "Theology after Dolly," *The Christian Century*, March 19–26, 1997, 285; see John F. Kilner, "Stop Cloning Around," *Christianity Today*, April 28, 1997, 10–11.
4. Martin E. Marty, "A Wolf in Sheep's Clothing," *The Lutheran*, May 1997, 27.
5. Philip Hefner, "Cloning as the Quintessential Human Act," *Dialog* 36, no.2 (summer 1997).
6. I. Wilmot et al., "Viable Offspring Derived from Fetal and Adult Mammalian Cells," *Nature* 385 (1997): 810–13.
7. James D. Watson, "Moving Toward the Clonal Man: Is This What We Want?" *Atlantic Monthly*, May 1971, 4.
8. "Cloning Animals—A Suitable Case for Concern," *Glasgow Herald*, February 25, 1997.
9. Karen Lebacqz, "Cloning: Asking the Right Questions," *Ethics and Policy*, newsletter of the Center for Ethics and Policy at the Graduate Theological Union (Winter 1997): 4.
10. Ryszard J. Chetowski, "Testimony before the Senate Select Committee on Genetics and Public Policy," American Society for Reproductive Medicine, Office of Government and Media Relations, Washington, D. C., April 1997.
11. Francis C. J. Pizzulli, "Statement on Human Cloning," California Senate Select Committee on Genetics and Public Policy, April 9, 1997.
12. Cf. Ted Peters, *For the Love of Children: Genetic Technology and the Future of the Family* (Louisville, KY: Westminster John Knox Press, 1996).

3

Saying No to Human Cloning

ABIGAIL RIAN EVANS

> A man of serious conscience means to say in raising urgent
> ethical questions that there may be some things that men
> should never do. The good things men do can be made com-
> plete only by the things they refuse to do.[1]

WITH THESE WORDS
Paul Ramsey confronts us with the central question about human
cloning: Is this a procedure we must refuse to do?

My answer is yes. We should refuse to practice human cloning
because it is morally wrong. I will offer four reasons for opposing
human cloning: (1) it is not a necessary solution to any human
tragedy; (2) it fosters a reductionistic rather than a holistic view of
human nature while treating people as means not ends; (3) it un-
dermines the structure of the family and human community; and
(4) it creates a pressure to use this technology and make it a god.
Each of these reasons, I point out, is grounded in the theology of
the Reformed tradition.

The speed with which the field of genetics has expanded is
dizzying. Progress in science, of course, has offered many benefits
over the course of human history. It has cleared up many miscon-
ceptions, removed illusory sources of fear and groundless super-
stitions, and helped us to understand the wonder of our bodies and
our universe. Technology has removed much of the danger of life
and enabled us to conquer some previous limitations and barriers
to a full life. All of this, however, has been a mixed blessing. By
displacing the categories of spirit and of a transcendent God with
material categories and depersonalized machines, science has left
us powerless in the arena of the deeper questions of life, the questions of purpose, love, and meaning.

Meanwhile, ethics straggles behind. The poverty of our ethics is reflected especially in the very words we use for the creating of human life. We have moved from talking about genesis (to begin), which the Greeks used to connote the springing forth of new life, to the word procreation, with its reference to humanity's cooperation with a creator God, to the term reproduction, a metaphor of the factory, foreseen in Huxley's *Brave New World*, to test-tube babies and now the possibility of replication by cloning.[2] For many of us the most troubling realm of genetic engineering is the reproductive area. As Leon Kass has expressed it, "Thus engineering the engineer as well as the engine, we race our train, we know not where."[3] Birth becomes a medical event instead of a family celebration; it even becomes a commercial enterprise at $10,000 per in vitro fertilization (IVF) birth. Right now the United States is one of the few countries in which you can sell human sperm and eggs.

At the same time, we must be careful not to outlaw or restrict potentially positive scientific developments with overly prohibitive legislation aimed at aspects of cloning which we do not support or condone, such as human cloning. The real value of the technical breakthrough that was achieved in Scotland is that it could lead to cures for some of the most horrible diseases we know. Breakthroughs in organ transplantation, cures for Parkinson's disease and cystic fibrosis, and inexpensive lifesaving therapy for hemophiliacs are just a few of the imaginable benefits. Can we support plant and animal cloning while opposing human cloning? Interestingly enough, Ian Wilmut, the chief researcher on the cloning of Dolly, has stated that the cloning of animals such as sheep is acceptable, but that no human cloning should ever be allowed.

Well-meaning ethicists and theologians may differ on these issues. But no matter how diverse our religious positions, we who are people of faith still have more in common with one another than with those who operate from a mechanistic, technocentric worldview. One of the most important grounds of commonality between religious traditions is the pastoral dimension of these decisions. How might new technologies like cloning affect marriage, the family, and the human community?

The foundation for my opposition to cloning is rooted in core principles of Reformed theology that are especially germane to genetic engineering and specifically to reproductive technologies. These include the sovereignty and omnipotence of God; the dignity and worth of every person, however sinful, as well as our freedom and responsibility; the communal dimension of human nature; and the stewardship of life. From these theological principles, I draw my four reasons for opposing human cloning, which I will summarize in the remainder of this essay.

1. Cloning is not a necessary solution to any human tragedy.
When we consider the suggested goals of human cloning (to create spare body parts, produce a child, or advance science), in each case there are other techniques available to achieve these goals. If we use a utilitarian risk/benefit ratio, which is a common criterion for assessing scientific protocols, it is clear that the risks of human cloning, both biological and moral, far outweigh the benefits for individuals and society as a whole. If our genetic diversity is at peril and the family is threatened, these risks are too great. Science should be in the service of the most noble goals for humanity. Technology has sometimes used any means to achieve the end of a desired product or procedure, whereas Protestant theology emphasizes that both the means and the end are of moral significance because they affect individuals and the created universe.

2. Cloning fosters a reductionistic rather than a holistic view of human nature while treating people as means rather than ends.
The desire to clone another person is predicated upon a perspective that reduces men and women to their biology and that views them as instruments to be used in fulfilling their progenitor's purposes. The concept of replication of another person suggests that we are simply the sum of our genes, lacking uniqueness and the qualities which are part of being made in God's image. The word replication is antithetical to an integrated understanding of personhood.

Ultimately, theology's contribution to the cloning debate revolves around what it means to be human. From the Jewish and Christian perspective, our vision of a man or a woman is that of a unity of body, mind, and spirit made in God's image, created to live in relationship to God and others. There is a reciprocal relationship between the three parts of our nature. Christian theology teaches that the immaterial soul during a person's life unites with the material body in an indissoluble, substantial way. It has an analogical relation to the union of the human and the divine nature in Jesus Christ. We can observe the influence of one dimension of the human entity on another dimension. We err gravely in defining a human when we take one of these dimensions and make it the whole or when we separate the dimensions from one another.

Our contemporary analysis of men and women eradicates our spiritual aspect or at best relegates it to the theologians. The Hebrew attitude toward human personality, upon which the Christian view is based, was very different from the Greek dualistic understanding. The Hebrew word *nephesh* means "principle of life." Man/woman is body animated by this "principle of life." There was no immortality of the soul, or immortality of the *nephesh*. Another word used in the Hebrew scriptures is *ruach*, signifying a divine inbreathing. This spirit means breath, life, wind, vital principle of life, or source. Our spirit pervades every aspect of our nature. There is a profound sense of the unity of humankind which comes from the unity of God.

Our spiritual nature motivates and enables us to search for meaning and purpose in life and provides an integrative force in relation to our mind and body. Spiritual courage, for example, may enable people to transcend physical handicaps and suffering and to interpret them within the context of a deeper positive meaning. This is why simply looking for ways to eliminate certain "defective" genes will not necessarily ensure better people.

With this vision of what we should be, we are confronted with what we are—broken and imperfect. Our image is distorted, like a reflection in a cracked mirror. In theological terms, we label this brokenness sin. We have a tendency toward evil, but have the capacity to do what is good. Protestant theology in particular would say that man/woman has a propensity to run headlong into ventures without caution to the consequences. Reinhold Niebuhr expressed this in terms of our infinite capacity for self-deception. This recognition that we are not all we could be is crucial in relation to the pursuit of various reproductive options. Perfection will never be possible because the impediment is within ourselves. Hence we will simply replace one disease or imperfection with another.

Analyzing human beings in relation to our three-part nature is not sufficient in itself, therefore, for understanding the full Jewish and Christian perspective. A full or communal view means that we also see ourselves in relation to our social environment as social beings. We are defined not only by our internal workings but also by our social relationships.

Western society has too long neglected the communal dimension of human nature. Especially from the Jewish perspective, seeing man/woman as part of the community, as the nation of Israel, was crucial to understanding each person as an individual. Carried into the Christian tradition, this communal view of our human nature was reflected in the image of the church as the body of Christ. The Reformed doctrine of the priesthood of all believers sees every person as a priest to every other; the dignity and worth of persons is within the community. We are interconnected as one human family. If cloning were universalized it would threaten this communal dimension of the human family.

This theological vision of our humanity, which includes our dignity and worth, demands that we each are seen as inherently valuable. The dignity and worth of each person is grounded in the Christian teaching of the equality of all persons and reflected in the Kantian dictum to treat persons as ends in themselves and not simply as means. In terms of genetic engineering, this teaching prohibits using one or more individuals specifically for experimental purposes simply to advance science, unless they are freely and fully informed and choose to participate. Women are especially at risk of being devalued, of providing a "rent-a-womb" service. It took 277 tries to clone a sheep. How many tries would it take for the first human clone? And what of the women used? Note, for example, that in the celebrated case of Mary Beth Whitehead, the surrogate mother, against William Stern for Baby M, the presiding judge referred to Ms. Whitehead as an "Alternative Reproductive Vehicle." Some feminists blame scientists for robbing women of motherhood by moving birth from the womb to the laboratory.

Cloning tries to force an outcome on the individual—to fulfill a predetermined destiny that the individual may not be able to fulfill. In fact, if the individual pursues another destiny because his or her interests and gifts are different from what is expected by those doing the cloning, the very uniqueness of the individual may be undervalued. The principal problem with cloning individuals with so-called desirable traits is that, even if we agreed about what the traits were, we would not be able to predict the environment necessary for a given genotype to produce the same phenotype. However, even if we were successful, the world of the past in which the clones matured may not be adaptive to the world a generation hence. As Leon Eisenberg suggests, "[T]he traits which lead an individual to be creative or to exhibit leadership at one moment in history may not be appropriate at another."[4]

Another aspect of what it means to be fully human is our awesome freedom and responsibility. This truth is amply illustrated by the Parable of the Talents, in which the man who buried his talent in the ground instead of using it in service of humankind was cast into outer darkness (Matt. 25:14–30). Part of being responsible is cooperating with a creator God—not retreating into passivity.

3. Cloning undermines the structure of the family.

The similarity between cloning and IVF is recognized by researchers such as neurobiologist Lisa Geller, who says that intellectually she sees no difference between IVF and cloning, even if the latter makes her feel uncomfortable.[5] Among the underlying issues concerning IVF is whether any technical assistance in procreation is acceptable and whether parenthood is a right, entitling couples access to various reproductive technologies. Many of the reasons to oppose IVF, when surrogate mothers are used, apply to human cloning, since a host woman is needed.

Most of the new reproductive technologies separate love, the conjugal act, parenting, and family. Surrogate motherhood carries this separation one step further by introducing a third person. Somehow, disembodied elements such as impersonally donated sperm and egg are less intrusive emotionally to the unique relationship between one man and one woman. I am not necessarily objecting to all technical assistance in reproduction, but it is interesting to observe that surrogate motherhood contracts were ruled illegal because of the abuses that are believed to exist. Cloning may also introduce an outside person into the birth process. It even raises the question whether terms like "baby" and "birth" apply. Parenthood becomes redefined, and no male is necessary in cloning. Neither are love or sex. Reproduction and progeny are not connected. Furthermore, cloned individuals may have difficulty determining who their parents are.

4. Cloning creates a pressure to use this technology and make it a god.

As the biologist Bentley Glass has pointed out, technology tempts us to be both Prometheus and Pandora. Every Pandoran advance in technology opens the box to disadvantages, so like Prometheus, who was blind to the long-term effects of the knowledge he stole, we must create remedies for our technology. Daniel Callahan observes that "we are at the mercy of these technological developments. Once they're here, it's hard to turn back."[5]

George Will, the syndicated columnist, describes the specter of cloning in which "narcissism and megalomania" are joined in the desire to replicate oneself.[7] Suzuki and Knudtson, in their 1989 book *Genethics*, discuss the need for ethics to guide the new genetics and suggest that humility toward our scientific discoveries may be the most appropriate attitude. Our need for humility stems not only from the potential risks of genetic engineering to plants, animals, and human beings. The greatest risk, Suzuki and Knudtson point out, arises from our hubris, our false sense of scientific mastery over our genes, while we ignore the still staggering limitations to our knowledge of human inheritance.[8]

As we speculate whether there will be research projects to clone humans, we note that research even at prestigious institutions may proceed unapproved and unregulated. Such was the case with the research at George Washington University on embryo-splitting conducted by Jerry Hall, Robert Stillman, and others. The researchers' stated purpose was "to help infertile couples by reproducing nature's ability to reproduce twins."[9] Perhaps the most interesting feature of this case was the researchers' belief that they were not beholden to their Institutional Review Board for approval prior to proceeding. Their defense was that the merit of the research could stand on its own.

One of the main ethical questions that the genetic engineering debate raises is whether one procedure leads inevitably to the next one. Once a particular technique is approved, does it later lead to its inappropriate use? Due to the rapid pace of human genetics research, funded by the federal Human Genome Project, we are able to test for the presence of a growing number of genetic disorders. So pregnant women may feel that they are being coerced not only to have amniocentesis (a prenatal diagnosis of some genetic disorders) but to abort fetuses that are found to be nonviable, genetically compromised, or unwanted by virtue of their sex or inconvenience.

All new options create a strong inclination to use them. Transplant technologies require people to justify refusal to be either a recipient or a donor. Life-support systems require dying persons and their families to justify either using or refusing those options. The ethical difference between sustaining life and hastening its end does not affect the burden of choice and justification. As an example, fetal monitoring and amniocentesis are often required for women over 35, whether they want it or not. We could even demand that a brilliant scientist with a fatal disease which will shorten his research career clone himself to carry on the experiments. (As pointed out, this is faulty science because there is no predicting that our clone will in fact be a scientist.) In all these instances, options compromise freedom.

In regard to correcting "defective genes," the concern is who decides what constitutes "good" and "bad" genes. Jeremy Rifkin, the major public organizer of opposition to any genetic engineering, claims that the approval of nontherapeutic gene replacement or genetic engineering of plants and animals will lead inexorably to the breeding of a super race where so-called genetically defective fetuses or potential parents who carry "defective genes" will be eliminated or sterilized.

Although I have problems with Rifkin's tactics, in which every conversation on the issue turns into a press conference and in which sloganism and emotionalism cloud the debate, his central point of looking down the road before we approve technologies is wise. For example, the decision to standardize the in vitro fertilization technique that uses donor sperm (AID) was scarcely discussed at all (except by the Roman Catholic Church). The general public has not generally regarded this technique as raising a moral issue.

Underlying the rapid growth in reproductive technologies is the belief that every person, whether single, gay, old, young, or married, has a right to be a parent. Hence science's job is to make that possible. This view is clearly represented by John Robertson, who concludes that cloning by embryo splitting has fewer risks and more benefits than first appeared and would be ethically permissible in most cases.[10] As Richard McCormick points out, Robertson's argument is based on the premise that anything that is useful for overcoming infertility is ethically acceptable.[11] At the heart of this pressure to use a technology is our tendency to make it our god. It is not so much that we play God when we practice high-tech medicine, but that technology becomes our god.

We would do well to remind ourselves of John Calvin's claim that the purpose of life is "to maintain humanity among individuals." Life is not just a question of private ethics. It is also a question of public morality. The ultimate criteria for any technology are these: How do we glorify God, recognize God's sovereignty, honor each person's dignity, practice stewardship of the earth, and enhance life to the fullest? Human cloning fails to meet these criteria adequately. It should be banned.

NOTES

1. Paul Ramsey, *Fabricated Man: The Ethics of Genetic Control* (New Haven, Conn.: Yale University Press, 1970), 122–23.

2. Abigail Rian Evans, "Genesis, Procreation, or Reproduction," in *The Church and Contemporary Cosmology*, ed. James B. Miller and Kenneth E. McCall (Pittsburgh: Carnegie Mellon University Press, 1989), 323–44.

3. Leon Kass, "The New Biology—What Price Relieving Man's Estate?" *Science* 174 (November 19, 1971): 785.

4. Leon Eisenberg, "The Outcome as Cause: Predestination and Human Cloning," *The Journal of Medicine and Philosophy* 1 (December 1976): 323.

5. Lisa Geller, quoted by Jeffrey Kluger, "Will We Follow the Sheep?" *Time,* March 10, 1997, 70.

6. Daniel Callahan, quoted by Kluger, "Will We Follow the Sheep?" 72.

7. George F. Will, "The Moral Hazards of Scientific Wonders," *Washington Post*, February 26, 1997, A19.

8. David Suzuki and Peter Knudtson, *Genethics: The Clash between the New Genetics and Human Values* (Cambridge, Mass.: Harvard University Press, 1989).

9. Ruth Macklin, "Cloning with Prior Approval: A Response to Recent Disclosures of Noncompliance," *Kennedy Institute of Ethics Journal* 5 (1995): 57–60.

10. John A. Robertson, "The Question of Human Cloning," *Hastings Center Report* 24 (March–April 1994): 13.

11. Richard A. McCormick, S. J., "Blastomere Separation: Some Concerns," *Hastings Center Report* 24 (March–April 1994): 14–16.

4

Cloning and the Moral Imperative

SIR JOHN POLKINGHORNE

■■■■ THE BIRTH OF THE ■■■■■■■■■■■■■■■■■■■■■
cloned sheep Dolly, achieved by scientists at the Roslin Institute by taking the nucleus of a cell from the udder of an
adult ewe and inserting it into an egg cell from which DNA
had been deleted, has been both a remarkable scientific
breakthrough and the trigger for much discussion about the
ethics of genetic engineering. The public response has largely
neglected the immediate benefits likely to accrue (the ready
production of therapeutic proteins in the milk of transgenic animals and—in the somewhat longer term—the further improvement of animal herds) and instead concentrated on much more
speculative and disturbing scenarios. Most notably, these have
included the cloning of human beings, despite the fact that the
most likely immediate human consequences resulting from
the Dolly episode will be benefits for research into aging and
tissue regeneration, deriving from an improved understanding of how genes are switched on and off in particular cells
of the body.

It is the supposed threat of the "Mad Scientists" and their
"Unscrupulous Employers" that has caught the public imagination. Beneath the science fiction and the exaggeration, however, there are very serious questions to be considered and they
are all the more timely, and liable to receive judicious and careful discussion, because the technology is not yet available to be
pressed into use. Theology's concern with creation and with individual human identity and value means that it should be in a
position to make a significant contribution to the debate.

Animal Cloning

Because the world is God's creation, all the elements that make it up have an appropriate value and attain a corresponding ethical status. In the case of sentient animals, this implies a respect for life and a moral obligation on humans not to inflict suffering beyond strict limits and for proportionate ends. There are, of course, differences between the world faith traditions, and within the Christian tradition itself, about exactly what these ethical requirements imply and where the boundaries are to be drawn. Most Christians accept the use of animals for food, subject to proper husbandry and humane slaughter, and most also accept the carefully controlled use of animals in scientific and medical experiments undertaken for serious and beneficial ends. There is, therefore, an ethically acceptable degree of instrumental use of animals by human beings, just as in the created order there is an instrumental use of living beings by other living beings in the food chain that sustains life on earth.

The experimental work that led to the birth of Dolly seems to find an acceptable place within this general understanding. There was a high wastage rate (277 attempts resulted in only one success), but that is only to be expected in pioneering a new technique. The purposes for which the research was undertaken were certainly serious and significant. It does not seem that a totally new ethical issue arises as far as animal cloning is concerned. Human cloning is a different matter altogether.

Human Cloning

The Abrahamic faiths (Judaism, Christianity, Islam) attach a unique and continuing moral and spiritual significance to the individual person. This derives from the status bestowed on each human creature by the Creator, as the personal object of divine love and compassion. An immediate ethical corollary of this theological understanding is that no human being is available for instrumental use of any kind. Beyond the community of those who share this religious insight, there is also a wide acceptance of the same moral stance, for it can be held to follow from the recognition of the intrinsic dignity and worth of human nature in itself. Such an understanding finds expression, for example, in the rule of medical ethics that experimental treatments should only be used on patients with their informed consent and with the benefit of that individual patient being the ethically controlling consideration. The mere fact of the permissibility of animal cloning in certain circumstances can, therefore, carry no immediately transferable implication for the moral permissibility of deliberately cloning human beings.

Human clones have always existed, however, brought about by the natural process of the birth of identical twins. The way in which that happens is, of course, entirely different from the way used to produce Dolly, for identical twins originate in the separation into two halves of a very early embryo developing in utero. However similar such twins may be in appearance and some other traits, there is absolutely no doubt that they are two separate individuals whose lives and personalities may develop in markedly different ways. If people had been willing to pause for a moment to take in this simple fact, it would have put to rest much of the wilder speculation that erupted with the account of the existence of Dolly. A clone derived from a dead child, or a dead parent, would not in any way be the restoration of the person who had been lost to death. It would be a new person altogether. A clone of Adolf Hitler might well have grown up to be an industrious house-painter and not a second dictator. There is no simple genetic determinism of who we shall be. One of the by-products of the furor about Dolly has been to remind thoughtful people of the poverty and implausibility of a genetic reductionist account of human nature. The note of genetic triumphalism has become somewhat muted, though apparently Richard Dawkins thinks it would be "mind-bogglingly fascinating" to watch a younger clone of himself growing up.

Instrumentality

The wilder shores of the scientific response to the news about Dolly produced some frankly instrumental suggestions of a peculiarly morally repulsive kind. Among them were references to the possibility of "restoring" lost relatives. Quite apart from the fallacy we have already noted as present in this proposal, it would be the procreating of a person for reasons wholly detached from that person in his or her own self. The burden of "being" that lost relative would be a deeply psychologically damaging imposition on the child thus brought into existence. In the sight of God, no one is a substitute for anyone else; each of us possesses value simply by being ourself and no other.

Equally unacceptable, because equally instrumental, would be bringing a person into being with the intention of producing as close a genetic match as possible for someone who needed a "spare part" (kidney, bone marrow, etc.). It is possible that some parents try to do this by natural means if they are faced with the profound problem of caring for a child with a serious congenital defect. Once again, it would be very psychologically damaging for a child even to suspect that he or she owed their existence primarily to the duty to help a sibling, rather than for the sake of the value and worth of their own being.

The moral case against any form of instrumental cloning of human beings, including the eugenic multiplication of "superior" types, can be summed up in the Kantian maxim that human beings should always be ends and never means. For the religious believer, the foundation of that maxim lies in the belief that every human being is a creature made "in the image of God" (Gen. 1:27).

Further Issues

Some further issues of theological significance are connected with the question of human cloning:

1. "Playing God"
Whenever a scientific advance offers the opportunity for some novel kind of human intervention in the order of nature, there will be voices raised to oppose the procedure on the grounds that it is inappropriate for human beings to exercise powers that rightly should be reserved for God alone. The assertion is made that going ahead would amount to attempting "to play God."

In a literal sense, this is obviously a theological absurdity. The Creator holds the world in being, moment by moment, preserving it from falling back into the abyss of nothingness. This is the primary meaning of the doctrine of creation out of nothing or *creatio ex nihilo*. It certainly does not mean that sometime in the past God formed the universe out of a curious kind of stuff called *nihil*, but rather that at all times the world exists solely because of the divine will that it should do so. In the Hebrew Bible the word *bara* is used for divine creating, while the common word *'asah* represents human making, including, by implication, the discoveries of science.

There is a proper sphere for the latter. There has been much theological discussion about what might be meant by the Creator's granting to humankind a "dominion" over nature (Gen. 1:28), the suggestions ranging from a Baconian kind of license to exploit to a much more caring stewardship of natural resources. Such "dominion" must surely include allowing a significant degree of intervention into natural processes. There is no theological requirement simply to let nature take its course; otherwise the whole practice of medicine and surgery would be religiously unacceptable (cf. Ecclus. 38:1: "Honor physicians for their services; for the Lord created them"). Human skill is God-given (Ex. 31:1–6). Jews and Christians are bidden to love the Lord their God with all parts of their being, including their minds (Deut. 6:5; Matt. 22:37). There is plenty of theological endorsement of the general project of scientific research ("reading the book of nature," as the seventeenth-century founders of modern science liked to say). However, it by no means follows that everything that could be done should be done.

2. "Reverence for life"

The coming-to-be of terrestrial life, with the eventual dawning of self-consciousness, so that in humanity the universe has become aware of itself, is the most remarkable event in cosmic history known to us since the big bang. Simply at the scientific level of understanding, this should induce in human beings a great respect for life. We have already seen that the doctrine of creation endorses this insight. The widespread acknowledgement of the ethical status and moral worth of individual persons is similarly theologically undergirded.

Not so readily agreed, however, either secularly or religiously, is the question of at what stage of fetal development the human person can be recognized as being fully present. In its Report to the British Government on the way in which research into human embryos should be controlled and regulated, the Warnock Committee showed that it is possible to reach widely agreed moral conclusions without having to settle, to universal satisfaction, such difficult and disputed matters as the onset of full human moral personhood. The Committee proposed that, at the very least, the human embryo was entitled to a profound ethical respect by virtue of its possessing the potentiality for full human development. On this basis, the Committee made the recommendation (now incorporated into the Statute Law of the United Kingdom) that no experimental procedure should be permitted to be carried out on an embryo beyond the age of 14 days from fertilization (understood as the time at which cell differentiation begins to appear with the "primitive streak").[1]

Not only does this episode relate directly to human cloning in the United Kingdom through its restrictions on embryo research, but it also has important collateral implications for the general consideration of cloning issues. It provides a clear example of what scientifically could be done (experimentation beyond 14 days) being held to be morally something that should not be done, precisely because of the very high degree of ethical respect to which any form of human life, at whatever stage of development, is held to be entitled. It is a clear implication of the Warnock Committee's deliberations that the experimental creation of human beings is morally unacceptable.

Experimental Human Beings

The only way to test the efficacy of the kind of technique used to clone Dolly is to implant the resulting embryo and see if its gestation proceeds to term and results in a viable birth. In the case of sheep, 277 attempts were necessary before success was achieved. There are still unresolved questions about how long such a clone will live and how healthy it will prove to be. If animal experiments of this kind go seriously wrong, it is always possible to halt them by the humane slaughter of the beast concerned.

An attempt to use a similar procedure to produce a cloned human person would undoubtedly also require a large number of trials before success was achieved and would involve similar uncertainties about long-term consequences. In contrast to the work that led to the birth of the first IVF baby, the procedures would be the result of radical human manipulation and not simply the facilitating of a natural process. Putting it bluntly, it would inevitably require the production of "experimental human beings." This, in itself, is morally unacceptable. If the profound respect due to an unimplanted embryo requires that experimentation cease at 14 days, how would a much more extended series of experiments in utero be ethically justifiable? These procedures might have as their intended end a desirable purpose, such as the birth of a healthy baby who might otherwise suffer from a severe mitochondrial disorder, but the manner in which this had become feasible, through a sequence of experiments of this kind, would have been ethically tainted. The end would no more justify the means than it would, say, in the case of a fetus conceived naturally but with the intention of providing suitable material for the treatment of Parkinsonism in a close relative.

If this moral conclusion is accepted, society will need to express its will in an appropriate kind of regulation. This could take a number of forms of differing potential flexibility: a statutory prohibition, a moratorium for a number of years, a code of practice. The seriousness of the moral issues involved encourages the consideration of a strict legal ban. Morality and the law are by no means identical, but they may be expected to coincide in cases of the greatest gravity (murder, sexual abuse, etc.). The protection of the ethical status of humanity is surely a matter that should be of concern to the law of the realm.

Conclusion

Not everything that can be done should be done. The technological imperative, encouraging the continuing pioneering of new techniques, must be tempered by the moral imperative, requiring that such techniques should be achieved by ethically acceptable means and employed for ethically acceptable ends. The search for wise decisions must involve the relevant scientific experts (for only they have access to the knowledge on which assessments of possibility and consequences can be based), but it cannot be delegated to them alone (for they possess no necessarily unique insight beyond the topic of their professional expertise). There must be other parties in the debate, which centers on the nature of the respect and restraint due to human life and to human moral dignity. Here theology, with its insight that the good and perfect will of God the Creator is the true origin of all value, has an important contribution to make. Theology will not seek to stifle advances that could benefit humankind in acceptable ways, but it will insist that the means by which these desirable ends are achieved must themselves be of ethical integrity.

Note: The author is a member of the Human Genetics Advisory Commission in the United Kingdom, but the opinions expressed in this essay are his alone and are not to be attributed to the Commission.

NOTES

1. House of Commons Select Committee on Science and Technology, "The Cloning of Animals from Adult Cells," (London: Her Majesty's Stationery Office, 1997).

5

A View from the Underside

PETER J. PARIS

SCIENTISTS HAVE
not been eager to offer enthusiastic support for the idea of human
cloning. For reasons that are unclear, several, including Dr. Ian
Wilmut, the progenitor of Dolly the cloned sheep, do not favor the
cloning of humans. Thus, unfortunately, the voices of scientists
have been noticeably absent from the public debate over the matter.

That absence not only invites curious and speculative rumi-
nations among interested nonscientists, but it also causes many,
including this author, to render negative judgments about the scientists in question. The apparent reluctance of the scientists to
transcend the boundaries of their science and discuss this novel
possibility robs the public debate of their specialized knowledge
and insightful counsel. Scientists are needed in the public discussion in order to keep the debate truthful about the facts and honest
about the interest of science in this particular pursuit of knowledge.
The voices of the scientists are needed in order to help the public
at large and ethicists in particular to see the possible benefits and
potential threats that human cloning could provide.

Unfortunately, those scientists who contend that human cloning
should not be undertaken seem disingenuous to the extreme. Even
though most have said that their reasoning is ethical in nature,
they fail to explicate it clearly. If their position is based on scientific reasoning, the public debate would be helped in knowing its
logic. If not, then scientists contribute no special moral weight to
the debate.

Clearly, the cloning of humans must require the agency of scientists skilled in the oversight of the relevant technology. As long
as most people view the good of science by its productive ends
and the degree to which social value is increased, as in the pre-

vention of disease and the maintenance and enhancement of good health, no moral problem arises. Thus, it would appear that, whenever the goals of science have been unquestionably humanitarian in nature, scientists have had no hesitation in publicly advocating their value.

In all such circumstances, however, the task of ethicists has centered on the moral quality of the means scientists have employed in their many and varied experiments. Drawing upon the cumulative wisdom of the ages and especially the United Nations Universal Declaration of Human Rights, various rules and guidelines have been derived to protect the inherent dignity and inalienable rights of human subjects used in scientific experimentation.

Not infrequently, the goals of scientific projects have been viewed by the public as immoral. Illustrations of such can be found among many classified research projects undertaken for military purposes. Under such conditions the protective cloud of governmental secrecy has prohibited public scrutiny of either the goal or the implications of the undertaking.

The so-called Manhattan Project that culminated in the production of the atomic bomb constitutes our most notable example of this genre. Germ and chemical warfare would represent another morally objectionable use of science. In general, science continues to be supported and justified by appeals to a utilitarian ethic which seeks the maximization of the good for the greatest number. Clearly, all quantitative goals of utility are morally problematic when viewed from the perspective of those who are actually or potentially vulnerable to being harmed by the project. Hence, we might be prone to ask those vulnerable Japanese citizens the following questions: "How does the science of nuclear energy appear to the survivors of the 1945 atomic blast on Nagasaki and Hiroshima?" or "Was the mass sacrifice of so many innocent civilian lives justified by the termination of the war?" Obviously, the relative few or the minority can expect little satisfaction from a utilitarian ethic, since it does seek the greatest good for the greatest number. Hence, the implications of popular reliance upon utilitarian thinking are ominous for racial and ethnic minorities.

Cloning and the Problem of Racism

Thus far, the public debate over human cloning has not attended to the impact of race and racism on the subject. This is surprising since the whole of American history has been shaped and organized by those principles of privilege and subordination. To ignore such an ubiquitous reality is both unwise and morally perilous.

Since slavery was justified for many centuries by appeals to utilitarian arguments and since various other contemporary human inequalities are justified similarly, it is reasonable to assume that scientists could be motivated to clone humans for ignoble purposes. For instance, might not the technology make possible the production of any number of use-objects of which an unskilled work force would be one? Given our terrible history of race relations, is it not conceivable that scientists might employ the science of breeding to produce a work force that would not only have a level of mentality thought to be appropriate for its functioning but might also be resistant to various types of toxins? In other words, the cloning of humans could result in the production of a group of people whom Aristotle and others viewed as "slavish by nature." Certainly such an outcome would greatly help in terminating the constant search by Western capitalists for cheap labor markets, to say nothing of other prurient uses clones could serve. Such ventures could be very lucrative for scientists, and when have scientists not been tempted by monetary rewards?

Let us not imagine that these scenarios are so extreme that it would be foolhardy for any serious-minded people to contemplate them. And let us not be so naive as to suppose that only "mad scientists" in science-fiction novels would ever entertain such ideas. From the perspective of racial minorities in general and African Americans in particular, nothing could be farther from the truth. Let us remember that science played a significant role in many major catastrophes humans inflicted upon one another throughout the twentieth century—catastrophes like the Holocaust, the bombing of Hiroshima and Nagasaki, the deliberate exposure of human beings to radioactivity, and the production of land mines that have maimed thousands of children in various parts of the world, to name only a few. Hence, trusting implicitly in the moral integrity of scientists and their experiments would be naive.

Many of us are all too aware of the infamous Tuskegee experiment wherein a group of African American men were deliberately deceived by medical scientists who for three decades withheld from them treatment for syphilis. In spite of a lack of evidence in support of their views, many observers continue to believe that several of the men were subjected to the disease by medical injection. President Clinton's recent apology to the survivors of that terrible experiment has made it abundantly clear that science does not have a clean record with respect to the exploitation of its subjects. There is no clear way for nations effectively to cause their scientists to internalize the virtues of intellectual honesty and moral integrity in protecting the personal dignity and human rights of all peoples at all times and in all circumstances. Clearly, an effective ban would require more force than the agreements and educational resolves of such international organizations as the United Nations.

Cloning and Diversity

Since some of the synomyms for the word "clone" are "replication," "imitation," "duplication," "copy," "second," and "double," it is conceivable that humans would be capable of defining human clones as quasihuman because they are derived from an original and produced by human technology in lieu of natural processes. If so, this would certainly place both the activity and the product of human cloning outside the realm of morality. It is because we regard them as less than human that we justify human domination of livestock and the making of them into mere objects of utility. Who is to say that human clones might not be treated similarly? And what effective means do we have to protect vulnerable human populations, like prisoners or the poor and impoverished people both here and abroad, from becoming either unwilling or unwitting participants in experiments that aim neither at improving their own well-being nor that of their respective communities?

Like many, I am apprehensive that cloning will reduce genetic diversity. In particular, I fear the potential threat that cloning in general presents to the natural diversification of our common world and its environment. Since Europeans and Euro-Americans have never been able to affirm the value of the world's darker races as equals, there is little reason to believe that their scientists would not seek to rid the world of some of its racial diversity by combining the science of eugenics with that of human cloning.

The production of human clones goes against nature in that the latter requires that the genetic structure of all human offspring be a composite of genes from two donors. In that way, nature assures diversity and helps overcome some of the inherent weaknesses in either donor. Thus, it follows that widespread cloning would lead to a gradual diminution in genetic quality.

In spite of my several fears and contrary to the opinions of numerous church leaders, as well as many religious ethicists, I do not support a ban against human cloning by any particular national government. My reasoning on the matter is simple. In my judgment, legal prohibition of scientific enquiry is both ineffective and retrogressive. As a medical doctor recently said to me in a personal conversation, "That genie is out of the bottle and it is too late now to stop it from having its way." Unfortunately, both politicians and religious leaders are all too prone to propose legislation to resolve controversial issues.

Since the technology of mammalian cloning may someday become fairly simple and inexpensive, a ban by any particular nation would not prohibit interested scientists from carrying out their work in some other location. Also, banning the practice weakens the quality of the public debate because it makes it very difficult for scientists who might otherwise advocate the practice to do so. Few scientists are willing to enter a public discussion as proponents of an illegal practice. Let me hasten to add, however, that my opposition to a legal ban on human cloning does not imply any disinterest in the promotion of a vigorous public discussion of the matter. In fact, I oppose the ban because of my deep interest in fostering such a public discussion. A legal ban brings closure to a public debate rather than stimulating it.

It is interesting to note that the National Bioethics Advisory Commission (NBAC) has recommended a five-year ban on human cloning primarily to allow scientists suffcent time to minimize all possible risks to prospective cloned children. The principle of "causing no harm to such prospective children" is an important one in medical ethics. Not surprisingly, however, the NBAC report astutely avoids the religious questions concerning the unique meaning of every human individual.

The possibility of human cloning provides an occasion for one of the most fascinating public discussions of all time. Few subjects have ever involved so many basic human concerns across such a broad geography of knowledge and experience. Human cloning raises many issues pertaining to the realms of religion, ethics, science, technology, politics, and law. Since none of these realms contains suffcent knowledge and wisdom to determine the proper course of thought and practice for each of the others, no just decision on the matter can be had apart from the knowledge and wisdom derived from every realm of public life. And since there is no unanimity of opinion in any of the realms, decision making about the morality of human cloning must be carried on in an open forum regulated by all the rules and guidelines for excellence in public debate. Foremost among those criteria must be the virtues of honesty, civility, and mutual respect, both within and between each of the above realms.

Once again, the human race stands on the threshold of a new era of infinite possibility. As with all human creations, this one is also fraught with many potential dangers. Yet the dangers attending such novelty need not lead us to impulsive acts of retrogression, either by legislative decree or by the demonization of our opponents. Rather, the fundamental question for us all is whether we human beings are capable of seizing the moment of creative opportunity and deciding how to make this new technology serve the well-being of humankind. Unlike Prometheus, no modern scientist has stolen anything from heaven. Rather, the capacity for knowledge has been graciously given to humanity by the omniscient and omnipotent Creator of us all, the one whose authority and being are not usurped even by the capacity of the creature to clone itself.

6

Genes, Justice, and Clones

KAREN LEBACQZ

███ PRESIDENT CLINTON ███████████████████████
has called for a temporary ban on cloning.[1] The Vatican has called
for a permanent ban on cloning.[2] What is at stake in all this banning of cloning? I wish I could say that it is a concern for women
and for how cloning will affect women's status in the world, but
it is not. I wish I could say that it is a concern for the poor and how
cloning will affect the status of the poor and the gap between the
"haves" and the "have-nots," but it is not. Vatican spokesperson
Gino Concetti wants us to be born "in a human way." The Roman
Catholic Church supports only "natural" reproduction. It rejects
artificial insemination, in vitro fertilization, and cloning on grounds
that they are "artificial." The church call is for a permanent ban on
cloning. President Clinton's concern is not whether cloning is "artificial"; his concern is not how we are born, per se, but the uniqueness of each life. Will cloning undermine our unique identity, ren-
dering any cloned human somehow vulnerable to loss of rights or
to unjust treatment?

The Arguments That Fail

Neither argument is compelling. Definitions of natural and artificial are susceptible to challenge. Does the intrusion of technology
automatically make something "artificial"? In that case, all hospital
births would have to be considered artificial. Indeed, Protestant theologian Phil Hefner claims that cloning is merely an "unsurprising
exemplification" of what we have known for a long time about ourselves: We are "created co-creators" who have already totally re-
arranged the life-forms that constitute our agricultural enterprises[3]
and therefore are only following our "nature" when we engineer

ourselves.[4] If what is "natural" to us is precisely to make and use the "artificial," then the distinction between natural and artificial disappears.

One need not equate natural and artificial, however. It suffices to note that human life has always been socially constructed. Biologically, for example, there are not simply "male" and "female" children, but multiple forms of human anatomy. Different cultures take this evidence and construct from it very different ways of understanding how many "sexes" or "genders" there are.[5] Even so fundamental a division as that between "male" and "female" may therefore be shown to be socially constructed. When something formerly considered as "natural" as biological sex can be shown to be a social construction, it becomes difficult to sort out what is "natural" and what is "constructed" or "artificial."

As for concerns about uniqueness of human identity, here I join with commentators who point out that DNA alone does not give us our identity. Identical twins—and, even more strikingly, conjoined twins such as Abigail and Brittany Hensel[6]—share more than a clone would share with its DNA donor. Twins share the same original egg—and possibly even the same body after birth. The egg into which nuclear DNA is implanted contributes intracellular organelles such as mitochondrial DNA, and its cytoplasm plays a role in programming the introduced nuclear DNA. Clones would share only the same nuclear DNA, and not this programming environment. Moreover, our genotype interacts with our environment throughout our lives. Genotype and phenotype are not the same, and any simplistic genetic determinism will not do. Since DNA alone does not determine human identity, sharing DNA does not mean that we lack individuality. Hence, if each twin—and even each personality of conjoined twins who share one body—is considered unique and protectable as a person with rights, then there is no reason to presume that a clone would not be unique and protectable as a person with rights.

Thus, the two major reasons that have emerged from religious and secular arenas as reasons not to clone a human can be set aside. Another concern is that cloning reduces genetic variability. While I take this to be a legitimate concern, it is a concern that would come into play only if cloning were to be used on a wide scale and were to replace rather than supplement sexual reproduction. Since most people are not likely to give up ordinary reproduction in favor of costly and painful alternative procedures, I do not foresee the day when humans would give up sexual reproduction on a large scale.[7]

A Remaining Paradox

Are there, then, any reasons left to oppose cloning that could or should be taken seriously? I think there are. Ironically, I think the reasons for opposing cloning that make the most sense grow precisely from the same soil that gives the most serious possible justification for cloning. These reasons center in the desire to have children "of our own" and the implications of supporting this desire. Consider the following scenario:

Sam and Kerry have been together for 14 years. Financially stable and still in love, they very much want a child. However, they have an infertility problem. They have considered adoption, but would very much like to have a child "of their own"—a child who carries their genes.

What would we allow Sam and Kerry to do in order to have a child "of their own"? Would taking fertility drugs be acceptable, even though it would enhance the chances of producing multiple embryos—a form of cloning? Would artificial insemination be acceptable? In vitro fertilization? What if nuclear cloning were possible? What if it were the only technique that would give Sam and Kerry a child "of their own"? To what lengths will we go to allow couples to have children who carry their genes?

In an essay that accompanied the Web publication of *Nature*'s articles on the cloning of sheep, Axel Kahn commented that the debate about cloning has paid too little attention to the "current strong social and psychological trend towards a fanatical desire for individuals not simply to have children but to ensure that these children also carry their genes. . . ."[8] Today's society, Kahn suggests, is characterized by an increasing emphasis on biological inheritance.[9] This emphasis has created pressure for all kinds of techniques to allow otherwise sterile couples to reproduce—artificial insemination, in vitro fertilization, ICSI (intracytoplasmic sperm injection), and so on. Cloning would be yet another extension of such techniques.

That Kahn is correct in his assessment may be seen from the work of John A. Robertson, a lawyer and outspoken advocate of "procreative liberty" as a fundamental right. Defining "procreative liberty" as "the freedom to reproduce or not to reproduce in the genetic sense,"[10] Robertson argues that it is a basic right because procreation is intimately bound up with our sense of who we are: "Reproductive decisions have such great significance for personal identity and happiness that an important area of freedom and human dignity would be lost if one lacked self-determination in procreation."[11] Thus, for Robertson, there is a right to have children who are genetically linked to us. Moreover, this right extends to encompass the use of technologies designed to assist us in that endeavor: "If procreative liberty is taken seriously, a strong presumption in favor of using technologies that centrally implicate reproductive interests should be recognized."[12] Thus, artificial insemination, in vitro fertilization, and presumably cloning would be encompassed as technologies that allow us to exercise the right to reproduce "in the genetic sense."

Interestingly, in his early work, Robertson drew back from allowing cloning to be encompassed under the right of procreative liberty. "Actions that aim to produce offspring that are . . . replicas of other human genomes (cloning) [do] not fall within procreative liberty," he declared.[13] While his stress on the right to technologies that enable couples to have children with desired genetic characteristics tended to push in a direction of support for cloning, he was uncomfortable with this implication. He rejected cloning as conflicting "with the values that undergird respect for human reproduction."[14] Specifically, Robertson's understanding of procreative liberty was framed around an understanding that couples would want normal, healthy children. These are the "values" that undergird human reproduction. Because Robertson saw cloning as "nontherapeutic" genetic intervention, not directly related to having healthy, normal children of one's own, he rejected it as part of procreative liberty.

In fact, Robertson is not opposed to cloning, per se.[15] The question for him is whether cloning fits under the rubric of reproductive rights. In a recent essay, he has argued that "replication" through cloning "might fall outside the bounds of reproduction as commonly understood in today's society."[16] Precisely because cloning involves replication of DNA rather than new combinations formed by the union of sperm and egg, cloning might not count as "reproduction" and therefore might not fall under "reproductive rights." However, Robertson does leave the door open to seeing cloning as part of procreative liberty, provided that it is genuinely procreative—that is, if the genome cloned is of the person herself or of her own offspring.

I propose that it is possible to construct a scenario in which cloning is genuinely procreative in Robertson's definition, and in fact in which cloning is the only way for a couple to have "normal, healthy children of their own." Suppose Sam and Kerry in the above scenario are both women. They are a lesbian couple, deeply committed to each other and now wanting to start a family. Cloning would allow them to use the DNA from one, implanting it into the egg of the other, thereby ensuring that all the basic reproductive material for their child was "theirs." In fact, cloning is the only technique that would allow them to ensure that all of the genetic material that goes into making up "their" baby comes from one or the other of them.[17] As a society, we have gone to great lengths to allow heterosexual couples to have children who are genetically "theirs." Will we do the same for lesbian and gay couples?

To my mind, this is a fundamental issue of justice. I come from a theological tradition, the United Church of Christ, that has committed itself to equal rights for everyone, including gay and lesbian people. So strongly do I believe in justice for gay and lesbian couples that, if there is, as Robertson asserts, a "right" to have children "in the genetic sense," then I think we cannot support artificial insemination, in vitro fertilization, and other techniques that allow heterosexual couples to have children who are genetically "theirs" without also supporting the development of techniques such as cloning that would secure parallel rights for lesbian or gay couples. Not to secure equal rights for lesbian or gay couples is to further disadvantage already oppressed groups.

Lesbian women in particular face discrimination and oppression. They are oppressed as women, and they are oppressed as people who have sexual relations with those of their own sex. They face employment discrimination, unequal treatment under laws that provide for employee benefits, discriminatory treatment by courts, physical violence, denial of insurance coverage, and many other forms of unequal and discriminatory treatment in a society that claims to treat all as equals. These discriminations are enumerated in Carol Robb's study of the economic effects of sex.[18] Because lesbians already live under the burden of these forms of discrimination and oppression, to allow the development of exotic technologies designed to permit heterosexual couples to have children "of their own" genetically but to refuse the development of technologies that would allow lesbian couples also to have children "of their own" genetically is discriminatory, unfair, unjust, and oppressive. It further burdens an already oppressed group. I have spoken strongly in the past against oppression,[19] and I cannot do otherwise than to speak against oppression again.

If there is any legitimate use for cloning, then, it is precisely to extend to lesbian (and possibly to gay[20]) couples prerogatives and privileges that are already extended and taken for granted by heterosexual couples in a heterosexist world. At present, most lesbian couples do not have children. Many of these women would like to have children that come out of their committed love to another woman. Since cloning is the only technique that allows these couples to exercise a "right" to have children who are genetically wholly "theirs," if there is such a "right," justice might mandate support for cloning.

If we are uncomfortable about the implications of this argument, then perhaps it is time to step back and ask whether we have been wise in allowing the development of exotic technologies that allow heterosexual couples to go to almost any lengths in order to have children "of their own." In a world that groans under the weight of injustice, in a world in which children die of malnutrition by the thousands every day, in a world in which children's growth is stunted by chronic hunger, is there not something wrong with the quest for ever more and more exotic technologies to privilege the already privileged? Is there something fundamentally flawed with the notion that children must be genetically ours? Is the very language of "rights" out of place when it comes to procreation and families?

I think so. Yet, to challenge the notion that there is a "right" to children "of our own" puts us in the position where we might have to reconsider basic decisions that we have already made—decisions to allow in vitro fertilization, ICSI, and other techniques. Moreover, it puts us in the position where we might have to reconsider the ideologies that underlie those decisions—e.g., the notion that it is genetic links that make children "our own." This is risky business, for Robertson's arguments and those of other liberal theorists have already taken hold of the public imagination.

Cloning provides an ideal opportunity for us to challenge precisely the hegemony of such beliefs and their impact on our society. Who has gained the most from the development of in vitro fertilization? Is it children and the poor? Or is it those who are already well off and advantaged in society? Who will likely gain the most from the development of cloning? Alas, it is not likely to be gay men or lesbian women, who have already been excluded from the use of other exotic technologies. (Admissions criteria for in vitro fertilization clinics, for example, have often limited the technology to heterosexual couples.)

My sympathies, therefore, are with gay and especially lesbian couples for whom cloning might offer the possibility of having a child who is genetically "theirs." Yet when new reproductive technologies are assessed as practices, it can be seen that they generally do not advantage women, the poor, or children as a class.[21] Thus, I believe that it is precisely the disadvantaged men and women who would have the most "right" to the techniques of cloning—gay men and especially lesbian women for whom cloning provides the only means to have a child who is genetically "theirs"—who would be least likely to reap any benefits from the practice of human cloning.

As a matter of justice, then, there is a paradox here. Cloning is both warranted in order to extend privileges and rights to oppressed people and unwarranted in light of the fact that oppressed people are not likely to reap the benefits of cloning. Rather cloning will likely only re-create unjust patterns and practices that already exist with other exotic reproductive techniques. Our individualistic, "rights"-based assumptions about families and procreation need to be challenged, and fundamentally new understandings of family need to be developed, so that God's love for all children— especially those already born in circumstances of poverty and injustice—might be reflected in the human community.

NOTES

1. March 4, 1997; reported in the *San Francisco Chronicle* on March 5, 1997, p.1.
2. *The Washington Post*, February 27, 1997, A28.
3. Vegetarians, beware: The tomatoes you eat very likely have been engineered with animal genes!
4. Philip Hefner, Draft Response to the President's Commission on Bioethics, March 13, 1997.
5. See Karen Lebacqz, "Difference or Defect: Intersexuality and the Politics of Difference," *Annual of the Society of Christian Ethics*, 1997, at press.
6. "One Body, Two Souls" reads the front page of *Life* magazine (April 1996) in which the story of these twins is told.
7. Indeed, one of the jokes that circulated immediately after the announcement of Ian Wilmut's accomplishment went as follows: Cloning is reproduction without sex. What humans want is sex without reproduction, so cloning is not likely to be very popular!
8. Kahn is director of the INSERM Laboratory of Research on Genetics and Molecular Pathology at the Cochin Institute of Molecular Genetics in Paris. His comments can be found at http://www.nature.com/Nature2/serve...481 &CAT=NatGen&PG=sheep/sheep5.html.
9. Kahn's view is given credence by a recent television documentary that chronicled the tale of a family where the father had wanted children "of his own" and had assumed that it was his sperm that were being used to inseminate his wife. When twins were born with a blood type that indicated he could not be the biological father, he was so devastated that he was unable to accept them as "his" children. Eventually, husband and wife separated because he could

not reconcile himself to raising children who did not carry his genes.

10. John A. Robertson, *Children of Choice: Freedom and the New Reproductive Technologies* (Princeton, N.J.: Princeton University Press, 1994), 22–23; emphasis added.

11. John A. Robertson, "Liberalism and the Limits of Procreative Liberty: A Response to My Critics," *Washington and Lee Law Review* 52 (1995): 236.

12. Robertson, *Children of Choice*, 40.

13. Ibid., 167.

14. Ibid., 172.

15. John A. Robertson, "The Question of Human Cloning," *Hastings Center Report* 24 (March–April 1994): 6–14.

16. John A. Robertson, "Genetic Selection of Offspring Characteristics," *Boston University Law Review* 76: 421–82, at 438.

17. Because the egg into which nuclear DNA is implanted may affect the expression of that DNA, one cannot make exactly the same claim for gay couples as for lesbian couples. However, it is true that for both lesbian and gay couples, the nuclear DNA that would make up the child would be "theirs," whereas introducing either sperm or a non-enucleated egg into the reproductive process means that the nuclear DNA would not be "theirs" genetically.

18. Carol S. Robb, in *Equal Value: An Ethical Approach to Economics and Sex* (Boston: Beacon Press, 1995), Chapter 5: "Lesbian Identity."

19. See Karen Lebacqz, *Justice in an Unjust World* (Minneapolis: Augsburg Publishing, 1987).

20. The situation is a bit different for gay couples, since an egg is required for successful cloning. To the extent that the egg contributes mitochondrial DNA that may influence the development of nuclear DNA, we cannot claim that cloning would allow a gay couple to have a child whose entire complement of DNA is "theirs." However, it would allow them to have a child whose nuclear DNA is entirely theirs.

21. It is partly for this reason that feminists have been almost uniformly opposed to in vitro fertilization, in spite of the fact that it is touted as bringing new "freedoms" to women in the reproductive sphere. See, for example, Susan Sherwin, *No Longer Patient* (Philadelphia: Temple University Press, 1992) at p.132: "Whatever the actual motivation, the practice of IVF itself serves to accept and support the sorts of individualistic values that say it is fine to invest vast resources into reproducing a child of one's own genes, despite the unmet needs of millions of existing children."

7

Cloning the Human Body

STANLEY HAUERWAS AND JOEL SHUMAN

. . . now we are children of God, and what we will be has not
yet been made known. But we know that when he appears,
we shall be like him, for we shall see him as he is.

1 John 3:2 (NIV)

We know that the whole creation has been groaning as in the
pains of childbirth right up to the present time. Not only so,
but we ourselves, who have the first fruits of the Spirit, groan
inwardly as we wait for our adoption as sons, the redemption
of our bodies. For in this hope we were saved. But hope that
is seen is no hope at all. Who hopes for what he already has?
But if we hope for what we do not yet have, we wait for it
patiently.

Romans 8:22–25 (NIV)

In the circle of the human we are weary with striving, and
are without rest. Order is the only possibility of rest.

Wendell Berry

CLONING—
the nonsexual reproduction of an organism using the genetic material of another organism—has been a theoretical possibility for
some time. As such, it seems to have elicited very little in the way
of moral argument. Recent laboratory developments in mammalian
cloning indicate, however, that we soon may have the capacity for
human cloning, the nonsexual reproduction of the human body,
using the genetic material of another human being. This prospect
has evoked a loud and somewhat alarmed call for public moral debate, ostensibly to be led by "experts" in the field of bioethics. Our

imaginations, however, do not seem ready for such challenges. As a result, the first question we ask of them always seems to be, "Should we do what we now can do?"

We do not think we should do what we now can do. Christians, we believe, should resist the technological imperative that gives rise to such questions. However, we also think it a mistake to begin arguments about cloning with questions about whether we should do what we now can do. To begin in this way presupposes that we know who is asking such questions and why they are being asked. As a result, the politics producing the technologies that give rise to the questions are hidden from view.

For example, consider this sentence: "Our imaginations do not seem ready for such challenges." Who is indicated by the "our" in that sentence? Confronted by such an "our," Christians assume that we are included in the "our." As a result we—that is, we Christians—think we must then say what, if any, particular insights we have about these matters correlative to our convictions about God's created order or some other relatively benign set of beliefs. This is particularly challenging to Christians living in modernity who are afraid of appearing to be against human progress. After all, does not cloning promise to cure genetically carried diseases or even to eliminate human hunger? Surely Christians cannot be against a technology that promises such results simply in the name of not messing around in God's creation. Christians, especially given our relatively insignificant status in modernity, simply cannot afford another Galileo affair.

Such challenges certainly may need to be addressed, but we think to begin with such statements of the "problem" is to rob ourselves of the resources of the Christian imagination. In short, the question for us is not whether cloning is a good or a bad thing, but rather how Christians, given the character of the Christian community and in particular the way that community understands the human body, are to understand cloning. "Cloning" is not a new thing for Christians, since we believe we have been made part of Christ's body. But because the promised redemption of our bodies seems so slow in coming, we may be tempted to compromise the body we have in Christ by subjecting that body to biomedical technologies promising immediate relief from all forms of human suffering. Ironically, from the standpoint of the Christian body, biological cloning then becomes but another gnostic technique designed to avoid or to overcome our bodies as Christians.

This very way of putting the matter in fact challenges the presumption that what makes Christians Christians is the beliefs they hold. The same practices that have reduced Christianity to a set of beliefs freely chosen by the individual make cloning seem like such a humane technology. The modern presumption, formed by the practices of capitalism, that the "I" names a self apart from and reigning over my body also produces a Christianity that is mainly about satisfying my "I." In contrast to this view, we assume that what makes Christians Christians is that through baptism they are made part of Christ's body.

We believe, accordingly, that the question Christians must ask about nonsexual reproduction of the body is not whether it should be done, but whose body, exactly, should we be nonsexually reproducing? For Christians have for nearly two thousand years been about the business of nonsexually reproducing the one body that matters most, and indeed the only one that must be reproduced in pursuit of the human good, and that is Christ's body. We are part of a community of people comprised of many very diverse members that is itself that body, and we understand that it is our baptism and our discipleship as members of that body, and not the information encoded in our genes, that finally determines our lives.

The apostle Paul, though he was never tempted by the possibility of cloning, nonetheless saw the reproduction of his body as being essential to his life as a minister of the gospel. The body matters to Paul; he knew no spirit, no soul, and no self that existed apart from the body. It is in and through the bodies of Christians, he claimed, "whether by life or by death" (Phil. 1:20, NIV), that Christ would be made redemptively present to the world. This presence, moreover, was to be transmitted—or reproduced—in a very particular way, through a particular kind of pedagogy that is perhaps best understood as a profound friendship. "Whatever you have learned or received or heard from me, or seen in me," Paul wrote, "put into practice. And the

God of peace will be with you" (Phil. 4:9, NIV). Therefore Paul did not hesitate to exhort those in the young churches under his guidance to imitate him. For in that imitation he understood that the disciples were being formed into a body determined by something far more substantial than a DNA sequence. This is evidenced by the language he uses in corresponding with those troublesome Christians in Corinth, to whom he wrote:

> Even though you have ten thousand guardians in Christ, you do not have many fathers, for in Christ Jesus I became your father through the gospel. Therefore I urge you to imitate me. For this reason I am sending you Timothy, my son whom I love, who is faithful in the Lord. He will remind you of the way of life in Christ Jesus, which agrees with what I teach everywhere in the Church (1 Cor. 4:15–17, NIV).

This passage suggests that Paul not only expected his life to be imitated by those converted in response to his witness, but that he understood that this imitation would constitute their lives in a way so substantial that he freely used frankly "biological" language— the language of father and child—to express the relationship between himself and Timothy and himself and the Corinthian Christians. Our tendency as moderns is to make light of such language, to say that it is a "mere" metaphor for what Paul understood to be occurring in the "spiritual" realm—the realm of "belief." But to understand Paul's writing in this way is to weaken his understanding of the church by imposing upon him an incorporeal dualism he probably would have rejected.

Dale Martin argues that when we read Paul we need to leave behind distinctions between the physiological and psychological that we in modernity have come to accept as obvious.[1] Paul assumes the church is Christ's body in such a way that immorality is not *like* the body becoming ill or polluted; it *is* the body becoming ill or polluted. So questions of a man having sexual relations with his stepmother (1 Cor. 5:1), of Christian men visiting prostitutes (6:12–20), of eating meat sacrificed to idols (chapters 8–10), and of the proper eating of the Lord's Supper (11:17–34) are all connected. For Paul, each of these are questions of the purity of the body and consequently of the avoidance of pollution. A Christian man visiting a prostitute is the exact equivalent of the body being invaded by a disease that threatens all its members, since in fact every member is the body.

Paul understood that in this life there is no genuine spirituality that does not take the body seriously. Speaking as if things were otherwise, suggests Wendell Berry, tends to "imply that the Creation is divided into 'levels' that can readily be peeled apart and judged by human beings." Some version or another of this very compartmentalized view seems to prevail in modernity, and we typically understand the spiritual as another means of escape from the banality of the everyday. Against this perspective, Berry posits an alternative that clearly derives from his Christianity: "I believe that the Creation is one continuous fabric comprehending simultaneously what we mean by 'spirit' and what we mean by 'matter.'"[2]

Only when Paul is read in this manner do we understand the radical challenge he presents to the assumption that what makes us Christian and/or human is our "self-understanding." Paul really expected those converted by his preaching to display in their bodies the same way of life he displayed in his own. This expectation was rooted not in any sort of megalomania, but in Paul's faith that his body had been transformed by his baptism in so profound and so mysterious a way that he could not speak of that transformation except paradoxically: ". . . I no longer live, but Christ lives in me. The life I live in the body, I live by faith in the Son of God, who loved me and gave himself for me" (Gal. 2:20, NIV).

Paul's expectation that his body would be reproduced in the bodies of others was based on his understanding that "all of us who were baptized into Christ Jesus were baptized into his death. We were therefore buried with him through baptism into death in order that, just as Christ was raised from the dead through the glory of the Father, we too may live a new life" (Rom. 6:3–4, NIV). This is to say that Paul understood baptism into the church as the beginning of a process of transformative reproduction through which the Christian body would be "conformed to the likeness of his Son, that he would be the firstborn among many brothers" (Rom. 8:29, NIV). Paul knew that the body being reproduced in those he baptized and taught was not his own, but Christ's. In this sense Paul understood the body more thoroughly than those who see genetic cloning as being a sufficient means of reproducing the body. Really being a body, he understood, requires certain kinds of relationships with others. Berry makes a similar point in arguing:

> . . . the body is not so formally self-contained; its boundaries and outlines are not so exactly fixed. The body alone is not, properly speaking, a body. Divided from its sources of air, food, drink, clothing, shelter, and companionship, a body is, properly speaking, a cadaver. . . . Merely as an organism (leaving aside issues of mind and spirit) the body lives and moves and has its being, minute by minute, by an interinvolvement with other bodies and other creatures, living and unliving, that is too complex to diagram or describe.[3]

We believe that we are speaking here, lest anyone think otherwise, of the very moral issues that surround technologies of cloning. Berry's broad point is that our bodies are constituted by an extraordinary web of contingencies on a multitude of levels. What Christians should believe about the way these contingencies, especially baptism and discipleship, constitute the body seems not only consistent with what Wendell Berry is saying, but also analogous with the point the philosopher of science Michael Polanyi was trying to make in his critique of modern science's strong tendency toward mechanistic reductionism. Polanyi opposed the insistence of certain scientists that a thing's ontology lay not in its being a comprehensive structure functioning in a given environment towards a particular end, but in an analysis of its constituent parts. This view, he argued, although valuable in its place, is finally inadequate:

> Indeed, nothing is relevant to biology, even at the lowest level of life, unless it bears on the achievements of living beings—achievements such as their perfection of form, their morphogenesis, or the proper functioning of their organs—and the very conception of such achievements implies a distinction between success or failure—a distinction unknown to physics and chemistry.[4]

How this point is analogous to Berry's becomes clear when re-stated in explicitly theological terms: Any theological discussion of the human body, at any level, must include a consideration of the body's goods and the relationship of those goods to the high-est Good—its ultimate purpose—which is eternal friendship with God in the new creation. Such friendship is attained through the process of baptism into the life, death, and resurrection of Jesus of Nazareth, through which the body is transformed and made part of Christ's body, which is itself at once both an organism and a network of friendships which make Christ redemptively present to the world.

We cannot then speak of the body's goods—including the physical health of any one individual body—apart from its Good; for to do so is to attenuate the body's health, which cannot be properly considered apart from its relationship with other bodies. As Christians, we find our bodies taken up—"cloned," if you will—through baptism and discipleship into the one body whose presence the world cannot do without, a presence that affords the possibility of finally bringing order to chaos and giving rest from our striving in God's new creation. It is thus imperative that we continue first of all to reproduce that body—a reproduction that cannot be effected genetically—and to wait patiently for the final redemption of our individual bodies.

From this perspective biological cloning represents but another attempt at perfection in a world that no longer acknowledges God. No longer trusting in our ability to make sense of our sufferings through the sharing of our bodies with one another, we now seek to perfect our isolated bodies as if such bodies were intelligible in themselves. In the name of eradicating suffering, we use techno-logical power to avoid being with one another in illness and death. Cloning thus becomes simply another means to escape the knowl-edge that, when all is said and done, we will each have to die alone.

Ironically, the high humanism used to justify cloning as a means to overcome the limits of our condition as creatures repro-duces the very presumptions that are at the heart of the environ-mental crisis. When all life is seen to exist for the sole purpose of

serving *human* life, then humans presume that we can instrumen-
tally subject all life to our purposes. The widespread assumption
is thus that human cloning is wrong because it violates the uniqueness and the autonomy of the individual, but that cloning animals
is a fundamentally good thing insofar as it contributes to the elim-
ination of human suffering. But this assumption is highly questionable from the perspective we have developed in this chapter.

The redemption Paul says has begun in our bodies is cosmic.
Animals and humans are equally creatures of a good Creator, and
the ultimate purpose of both is nothing less than to praise God.
The idea that animals exist for no other purpose than to supply human needs and desires cannot be justified theologically. Given the
practices of the Christian community with regard to the body, we
can see no reason why Christians might think animals—much less
humans—can be cloned in the name of human progress. Any
"progress" that is not found in the joining of our bodies into the
one body of Christ, we suspect to be an idolatrous attempt to perfect the created order in a manner that denies our lives have already been perfected in Christ.

NOTES

1. Dale Martin, *The Corinthian Body* (New Haven, Conn.: Yale University
   Press, 1995).
2. Wendell Berry, *Another Turn of the Crank* (Washington, D.C.: Counter-
   point, 1995), 91–92.
3. Ibid., 94–95.
4. Michael Polanyi, "Scientific Outlook: Its Sickness and Cure," *Science* 125
   (1957): 480–84, at 482.

8

An Absence of Love

DAVID M. BYERS

■■ THINGS ON THE ■■■■■■■■■■■■■■■■■■■■
horizon are hard to make out clearly; they are dark shapes, nothing more. But set the scene in motion and they begin to change. Some, like threatening storm clouds, rise up quickly to engulf us. Others, like snow-capped mountains, rest serene in the distance, only gradually taking on color and stature as we approach. Others still, like a water mirage on a hot sheet of highway, recede before us, running out of reach, forever on the horizon.

What will people say of human cloning in the year 2100? That the technology broke furiously upon us, swept and confused us, left us breathless? That humanity approached it with calm grace, probed it wisely, decided to admire it and pass on? Or that it continued to shimmer in the distance, never any closer, barred by some unrecognized law of nature? Whatever we say of human cloning today is mere speculation, because it does not yet exist and may never exist. The creation of Dolly the sheep was far from easy; it took 277 tries to yield a single lamb. Moreover, Dolly is just mammalian, not human. Human embryos develop differently from sheep embryos; the genes in their cells "turn on" at different times. This difference may prove critical. As far as anyone knows, there are no human clones walking the streets now and there may never be.

But "what ifs" are fascinating, and we have every reason to ask them. Last year, the "what ifs" surrounded Allan Hills 84001, a meteorite, probably from Mars, that may or may not contain evidence of life. The implications of extraterrestrial life for our human self-image are so profound that whole conferences of sober-minded scientists, philosophers, and religious leaders were convened to discuss them. In the same way, we must talk about human cloning in the wake of Dolly's birth, since the technology could profoundly and rapidly change not only how we see ourselves but also who we are.

A fundamental distinction is in order before expanding upon this dramatic but quite defensible assertion. The phrase "human cloning," as used in this chapter, means the asexual replication of an individual human being at any stage of development. Human genes, cells, proteins, and tissues are routinely cloned for biological and biomedical research; they are useful for a wide range of purposes, from the treatment of burns to investigations of the way genes work to the quest for a cure for diseases like multiple sclerosis, cystic fibrosis, and hemophilia. Over the centuries, the Catholic community, represented most prominently by religious orders, has been one of the leading providers of health care in the world. Naturally, it applauds advances in medical knowledge that promise good without violating the moral law. The cloning of human biological material is not evil in itself and does not seem problematic when used for therapeutic ends.

One can argue that the knowledge of how to reproduce an entire human being asexually is also a good, and even that the individual technologies this knowledge produces may be beneficial. Understanding nuclear fission led to the development of nuclear weapons. However, it also enabled the creation of radioactive substances useful for medicine and (more controversially) made possible a way of generating electricity without burning fossil fuels. According to St. Augustine, the proper Christian stance is *fides quaerens intellectum*, "faith seeking understanding." Christians glorify God through their expanding understanding of nature, recognizing themselves more and more clearly as creatures in the midst of Creation.

The example of nuclear fission shows that the potential for mischief lies not in the knowledge, but in the uses to which it is put. Here is the sticking point for the cloning of an individual human. While the knowledge may prove a link to other important discoveries, or point the way to beneficent technologies undreamt of now, it is impossible to imagine any sufficient reason actually to clone someone. The Catholic theological and moral tradition, however respectfully it may view scientific advance, cannot justify taking this historic step.

This tradition would even suggest caution regarding the cloning of animals. Everyone already recognizes certain moral constraints in dealing with animals—avoiding all cruelty, for example. Cloning raises broader considerations, however. There may be consequences of cloning animal life (and, for that matter, plant life) we cannot now foresee. Moreover, what is morally permissible varies from species to species, depending on their circumstances and place in nature; cloning a simple organism is significantly different from cloning a cow or a chimpanzee. Finally, because we are creatures in the midst of creation, we have a responsibility to treat other species with respect, in the spirit of Sirach:

> All these things live and remain for ever
>   for every need, and are all obedient
> All things are twofold, one opposite the other,
>   and he has made nothing incomplete.
> One confirms the good things of the other,
>   and who can have enough of beholding his glory?
>   Sirach 42:23–25 (RSV)

Despite these constraints, Christianity has always posited a fundamental distinction between human life and all other creatures. Unlike some other perspectives and traditions, Christianity countenances the use of animals for human benefit. In principle, animal cloning can be considered an extension of classical breeding techniques, whether the object be saving endangered species, improving food production, creating useful pharmaceuticals in large quantities, or even generating organs suitable for transplantation in humans, all of which are presently possible. Animal models (a strain of mice, for example, that develop a particular human disease) are also extremely helpful in medical and other research. While the Christian view of animals has properly grown less casual that it was before, it remains essentially instrumentalist. Otherwise, Christians would all be moral vegetarians and would be forced to reject much scientific investigation.

Human Cloning

Returning now to the question of human cloning, we may anticipate that, while there is no sufficient or morally adequate reason for human cloning, surely some justifications will be offered. For example, clones could be useful for experimentation, since the researcher would not have to correct for individual genetic differences. Someone could have him or her self cloned in a new version of the search for immortality, or to have a source for "spare parts." Scientists or political authorities intent on "improving the human stock" could find cloning a wonderful tool for producing perfect children or accelerating the evolutionary process. The imaginative mind will no doubt discover other practical purposes for clones over time.

These justifications may seem cold and sterile, but experience teaches that people accommodate rather readily to horrors like the Holocaust or ethnic cleansing. Natural repugnance, a morality based on feeling, could not long withstand practical arguments in favor of cloning. Moreover, in a culture that prizes the freedom to do as one chooses, many apply moral repugnance only to their own behavior: "Well, I wouldn't do it, but. . . . " Over time, a generation or two perhaps, repugnance would dissolve into apathy and cloning would begin to "feel normal," as slavery felt normal to many Americans 150 years ago.

Only a morality based in conviction can help us handle the new questions a technological advance like cloning raises. Christians of different denominations will approach these questions from somewhat different angles, depending on their particular traditions. Perhaps all can find common ground, however, in the deceptively simple assertion that God holds each human being in a personal covenant, revealed in Jesus to be a covenant of love. We respond by worshiping God in a spirit that cries out *Abba*, "Father" (Gal. 4:6–7), and by loving others in the *imitatio Christi*. This theme runs throughout Scripture; take, for example, the quite straightforward assertions in John 15:8–17. Its most forceful expression is Jesus' response to the question "Teacher, which commandment of the law is the greatest?" (Matt 22:34–40).

We are, as far as we know, the only creature God created for its own sake, not to satisfy some other creature's wants and needs. Each human being has inherent dignity as a child of God, free to pursue his or her eternal destiny in relationship to the divine. At this most fundamental level, cloning is unacceptable because clones would be human beings created, at least in part, to fulfill the will of another human being. When a man and woman come together, they certainly hope to produce the perfect child, but do not aim to produce one with certain characteristics for certain ends. Even in vitro fertilization, which the Catholic Church resists on other grounds, is not employed to create a particular sort of child but to overcome sterility. Cloning would insert a new term into the equation of human reproduction, namely, a purpose for the offspring.

"Pre-implantation screening" is already in use to produce a baby free of a specific genetic disease. Consider, for example, a couple who know they are carriers of a genetic mutation that causes cystic fibrosis, and each of whose offspring therefore has a 25% chance of having the illness. They can produce an embryo from their own sperm and egg through in vitro fertilization techniques and subsequently have this single embryo "biopsied," teasing out one of the cells for genetic testing. Each of these cells is a cloned embryo in its own right, and of course it is destroyed in the testing process. If the "biopsied" cell is found to be free of the specific genetic disease, the researcher can assume the remaining embryo is free as well. The fortunate embryo—the remaining cells from which the biopsy was taken—can then be implanted. The rest, having served their purposes, can be discarded.

In the eyes of the Catholic Church, the cloned embryos are as fully human as the author of this essay; there is no reason to consider them anything else. From the moment its individual life begins, the new organism is unmistakably human from a genetic perspective. No scientific test will give another result; the clone is human. Moreover, it is an individual human which, if allowed to develop without interference, will grow and be born, live out its span of years, and, hopefully, receive the reward of a virtuous life.

This form of cloning, which is not future but present, suggests several related questions. We have already dealt with the first:

"May one clone a human embryo?" No, because these tiny beings are being created not to share freely in a covenant of love, but to gratify their parents' desire for a healthy child. Any not needed for this purpose are disposed of like trash. The second question is: "May one kill a cloned human embryo?" Again, the answer is obviously no. Those responsible for discarding "extra" embryos are engaging in an exercise of raw and lethal power over helpless innocents. Their brief existence is entirely at the will and whim of others, who call them into life and dismiss them again when they are no longer of service.

The fact that the testing occurs prompts a third question: "May one do research on, experiment with, or otherwise manipulate a human embryo, even a clone?" The answer here is a bit more complex, because it may be possible to intervene so as to benefit an embryo, curing it of illness or defect. The Vatican Congregation for the Doctrine of the Faith issued a document in 1987 titled *Instruction on Respect for Human Life in Its Origin and on the Dignity of Procreation*. The *Instruction* says experimentation on human embryos "constitutes a crime against their dignity as human beings having a right to the same respect that is due to the child already born and to every human person."[1] However, not every intervention is experimental. The *Instruction* quotes Pope John Paul II as follows: "A strictly therapeutic intervention whose explicit objective is the healing of various maladies such as those stemming from chromosomal defects will, in principle, be considered desirable [and] would indeed fall within the logic of the Christian moral tradition."[2] Medical science could appropriately intervene if the purpose of the procedure is to effect a cure and if there is a reasonable expectation of success. As noted above, Catholic teaching would treat the embryo as a member of the human community, a neighbor to be loved as oneself. It therefore condemns destruction or manipulation, while affirming attempts to heal.

The Ties That Bind Us

The *Instruction* raises another important issue. It strongly protests the separation of human reproduction from natural sex in marriage, and condemns in vitro fertilization and cloning for this reason. "Attempts or hypotheses for obtaining a human being without any connection with sexuality through 'twin fission,' cloning or parthenogenesis are to be considered contrary to the moral law, since they are in opposition to the dignity both of human procreation and of the conjugal union."[3] Every child should be the fruit of an act by which the parents give themselves to their partner in love and collaborate with the power of the Creator; procreation is another instance of that covenant that binds us to one another and to God. Moreover, "the good of the children and of the parents contributes to the good of civil society; the vitality and stability of society require that children come into the world within a family and that the family be firmly based on marriage."[4] Observing God's plan for human procreation leads to order and harmony; it is a foundation stone of what John Paul II calls "the civilization of love."

The Catholic Church would be as concerned about experimenting on and discarding embryos created with the technology that produced Dolly the sheep as with embryo splitting, because each clone, embryonic or adult, would be a human being. However, this technology raises issues that embryo splitting does not. For one thing, it represents a more radical intervention in reproduction. Instead of starting with an existing embryo and dividing it, the scientist produces an embryo using the nuclear DNA from an adult cell. Further, we know no more about clones derived from embryo splitting than we do about any other embryo; they share fully in the mystery of human variability. But the Dolly technology may allow science to reproduce a genetically identical copy or copies of an existing adult whose characteristics are already known. This creates a whole range of new possibilities: reproducing oneself for another generation; replacing a lost child; copying someone else's "perfect" child; cloning people with particular traits such as physical beauty, intelligence, or athletic ability; even creating new human subpopulations to serve as workers, soldiers, slaves, or prostitutes.

Not so fast, one could object; this is science fiction. If the technology proves to be feasible, however, clones may well be part of the human future. In mid-1997, the National Bioethics Advisory Commission proposed that the government ban federally funded cloning but permit privately funded (primarily commercial) laboratories to proceed, as long as they did not implant cloned embryos in women's wombs. From a Catholic perspective, this legitimates a "create-and-kill" mentality that will cheapen society's respect for life even further. From any perspective, the Bioethics Commission report makes the cloning question even more urgent and immediate. Clones are fine, the report seems to say, as long as they are not implanted. But how great a step is it then to say: "Clones are fine, why not implant them?" or even "Clones are fine and may have commercial or research value. Let's quietly implant some and see what happens"? Such a ban would invite what it seems to prohibit.

While the Catholic Church and other religious bodies will very likely urge world leaders to ban cloning universally and forever, this work may go forward anyway. If so, the church must be ready to offer guidance on how cloned human beings should be treated. It is not an idle exercise to imagine a world where child clones and adult clones join us in our ordinary pursuits, taking walks, buying groceries, giving lectures, selling insurance, handing down judgments in court or sitting next to us in church. How should we un-cloned individuals deal with such people? How should we deal with them if they happen to be clones of ourselves?

The first human clone, if there is one, will surely be treated as a freak. Considering the media attention the news of Dolly has received, the glare of the spotlight will fall much more brightly on that unfortunate person. Chloe—we will name the clone for ease of discussion—will grow up set apart, the object of tireless scientific and public curiosity, exposed to unending physical and psychological testing as she ages, to some degree a laboratory subject. And why not? Obviously, Chloe's principal value to humanity will be what science can learn from her. Will she have a normal lifespan? In what ways will she resemble and differ from her progenitor? How about her social relationships? How will she feel about her progenitor, who may be forty years older and simultaneously mother and identical twin sister? Who will take the place of her father? Then there are the legal questions. Who will be responsible for raising the child Chloe? Who will pay for her medical and other supervision, which will surely be enormously expensive, even if she is a healthy little girl? Will her progenitor be her legal guardian? Or will it be the U.S. government? Or a biotechnology company?

Such questions underscore the importance of the comments the *Instruction on Respect for Human Life* makes on the moral law, marriage, and the community. Human cloning would represent a radical shift in the ties that bind us. For the first time, we would have children with only one biological parent, and that parent would have contributed nothing more than a cell nucleus to the offspring. Moreover, all their siblings, if they had any, would be not only their identical twins but also twins of their parent. There has been much talk about nontraditional families in recent years, including models where the members are not biologically related. These groupings affect only a minority, however. The traditional family founded upon sexual love and reproduction is the only basis human society has ever known. Cloning has the potential to upset this "natural" pyramid, disrupting physical, psychological, and social relationships in entirely unpredictable ways. When Pandora opened her famous box, the one thing remaining after all the evils had flown out was Hope, cowering under the lid. Only a society with an iron-clad faith in progress would lay the ax of technology to its own roots.

Obviously, Chloe's life would be unusual in many ways, even in comparison with current international celebrities. If she is a "success," though, Chloe will not remain unique. As more clones appear, however gradually and with whatever controls, they will pose a new but familiar challenge for Christian theology and moral thought. The church will declare, as it must, that all clones have souls and must be treated with respect and love. They will be human individuals, equally the emanation of divine love, equally the subject of rights and responsibilities, equally called to the eternal salvation revealed in Jesus Christ. However, their welcome among us is far from assured. After confusion over identity and personal relationships, the greatest difficulty clones will face, and the greatest moral challenge they will pose, is social discrimination.

Clones will be different from nonclones, different from the rest of us. Many commentators have pointed out that clone and progenitor will be no more similar than identical twins, who share the same genome or genetic complement at birth, but develop differently because environmental factors and gene expression and mutation vary. That is debatable, if only because the genome of progenitor and clone will not start in the same place. The genome of the clone, when born, will be virtually identical to that of a progenitor who has already lived for twenty or thirty or forty years. Its natural capacity for variation may be less than that of twins. More importantly, the analogy with identical twins may hold only for progenitor and clone, or for two or three clones. Suppose a geneticist cloned Michael Jordan one hundred times. While the men would differ from one another, they would differ from other people more. Their individuality would be suspect, since they would be variations on a theme. People tend to see twins and triplets as interesting anomalies; they might see a hundred clones as a herd.

The two greatest commandments seek to remedy humanity's worst moral plagues: our lack of humility and our inability to get along with one another. We endlessly draw distinctions among ourselves, apparently by instinct. Moreover, we assign value to these distinctions; my group, it seems, is always better than yours. The drive to define and establish universal human rights encounters one form of discrimination after another: by sex, by race, by ethnicity, by age, by handicap, by beauty, by strength, by nearly anything that serves our pride and soothes our insecurity.

Even knowing that someone is a clone rather than "natural-born" would be enough to create a new class distinction. It would be impossible for multiple clones, and difficult even for a single clone, to conceal their status in this inquisitive age. Would the average middle-class Caucasian feel more comfortable with a Caucasian clone than with an uncloned African American? More inclined to respect the clone's rights, more inclined to socialize? Rejection and intolerance seem the likelier response. Consider, finally, that clones, while produced for defined purposes, would have free will. If they rebelled against their tailored fate, either as individuals or as a group, nonclones might see them as possessing no greater value than a spare embryo. The very last thing the human race needs is another cause for division, hatred, and war.

So many negatives. Are there no positives? There are, but not enough to strike a balance. Experimentation on cloned embryos may lead to therapies and cures that help other people. It will also increase knowledge of how genes work, which may have other benefits. Cloning, coupled with genetic engineering, may allow science to change humanity permanently in certain benign ways, eliminating diseases, giving us longer and more productive lives, perhaps increasing strength, longevity, even intelligence. From a theological perspective, one could speculate that cloning was a tool God had given us to build the Reign of God. A sober reading of history suggests that homo sapiens is making little progress toward that lofty goal. Perhaps cloning would enable us to speed evolution up, transforming ourselves into some successor species that is wiser and more virtuous. Perhaps we are merely a transitional form and cloning is the way to transcend ourselves.

These achievements, even if they were possible, would not justify cloning. They are not a sufficient reason for cloning, because they are illusory or purchased at too great a price. The price is not primarily the destruction of human embryos, shameful as it is. Cloning, at base, is an assertion of power over another human being, exercised without consent. Moreover, the cloner asserts power not just over the clone's liberty or privileges, but over its very being. The life and death of Jesus Christ, who did not deem equality with God something to be grasped at (Phil. 2:6–11), is witness against this addictive will to power. For the Christian, the critical consideration for human cloning has little to do with efficiency, with benefits for some, with scientific progress, even with a sense of cosmic adventure. Let this be the test: Would cloning be a loving act, not for the cloner but for the clone? We wish all babies were conceived in love and raised with love, even though experience demonstrates that many are not. If we cannot approach human cloning in the same gentle and humble spirit, then let us forebear. To paraphrase a famous prayer:

> Lord, grant us the serenity to accept the things we should not
> change,
> The courage to change the things we should,
> And the wisdom to know the difference.

NOTES

1. Congregation for the Doctrine of the Faith, *Instruction on Respect for Human Life in Its Origin and on the Dignity of Procreation* (Boston: St. Paul Books, 1987), 17.
2. Ibid., 16.
3. Ibid., 19.
4. Ibid., 24.

9

One Flesh?

Cloning, Procreation, and the Family

BRENT WATERS

▉ MOST RELIGIOUS ▉▉▉▉▉▉▉▉▉▉▉▉▉▉
responses to the prospect of human cloning concentrate on issues
emphasizing personhood or personal morality: Does cloning violate the unique identity of a person? Do I have a right to clone myself or another person? How would the clone feel? Although these
are important questions, the family is usually conspicuous by its
absence. This virtual absence of the family reveals much about
how we are coming to think about procreation. We tend to presume that parenthood is a private affair involving an expanding
array of reproductive choices. Given this presumption, it is only a
matter of time until cloning a living or dead person becomes one
among many reproductive options.

The purpose of this chapter is to suggest an alternative framework for thinking about human cloning, namely that of the family rather than individuals pursuing their reproductive interests.
Would emphasizing the family change what we perceive is at
stake in human cloning? In addressing this question, I will first
sketch what I take to be the emerging moral context for deliberat-
ing on human reproduction, and hence the setting in which we are
contemplating cloning.

The Principle of Procreative Liberty

John Robertson's principle of procreative liberty offers an illu-
minating depiction of how we are coming to think about human
reproduction.[1] According to Robertson, avoiding or pursuing reproduction is a fundamental right. It is a crucial freedom "because
control over whether one reproduces or not is central to personal
identity, to dignity, and to the meaning of one's life."[2]

There are three aspects of procreative liberty which need to be highlighted. First, individuals choosing to reproduce should have fair access to noncoital methods of reproduction. In what is described as "collaborative reproduction,"[3] a commissioning parent or parents utilize various combinations of techniques in conjunction with donated gametes or embryos in procuring a child. In this respect, there is no significant moral difference between natural and artificial methods in making a baby.

Second, personal reproductive decisions must be respected by others. Procreative liberty is a procedural principle reflecting the pluralist character of modern societies. Individuals holding differing, and often conflicting, values require procedures protecting them from unwarranted restrictions in exercising their reproductive rights. Every person should be free either to use or refrain from using available reproductive options. The only legitimate restriction, other than financing, is that the interests of commissioning parents, collaborators, and offspring should not be harmed.

Third, individuals have the right to exert quality control over the characteristics of their offspring. Since pursuing noncoital reproduction is a fundamental right, individuals may utilize various technologies in attaining not just any offspring, but desirable offspring. These interventions express parental care and affection, for preventing undesirable traits or enhancing desirable traits is a way of giving one's child a good start in life. If individuals are at liberty to procreate, then they also have the right to attain the kind of children they want or desire.

Now we may ask: When the technology for cloning humans is available, will it fall under the purview of procreative liberty? Despite Robertson's objections to the contrary,[4] I think the answer is yes. Robertson assures us that human cloning is so outlandish we need not trouble ourselves with its prospect. His objections have nothing to do with harming offspring. Rather, he asserts that cloning "may deviate too far from prevailing conceptions of what is valuable about reproduction to count as a protected reproductive experience."[5] In cloning we reach a point where attempts "to control the entire genome of a new person pass beyond the central experiences of identity and meaning that make reproduction a valued experience."[6] In short, cloning is objectionable because of a pervading quality which "violates a basic sense of what makes reproduction valuable."[7]

Yet his objection, presumably in the name of procreative liberty, begs the question: What is so different about the method or outcome of this technique that it should be prohibited? As Robertson admits, the reason is not that it harms offspring, but it is difficult to imagine who else would be harmed so long as appropriate safeguards are followed. Rather, he bases his objection on a more sweeping belief that cloning "deviates" too far from, if not "violates," the very "identity and meaning" of reproduction that make it a "valued experience." But what is this "meaning" of reproduction we would violate by cloning, thereby depriving it of its experiential value? Is this value or meaning found in the creation of a new or unique genome? If this is the case, what does this imply about the experiential value of identical twins or triplets? And why is it valid to impose this moral limitation at this particular point while dismissing any other such restrictions, other than harm, at other points along the spectrum of technologically assisted reproduction? Why is a normative claim about the "meaning" of reproduction abruptly inserted into a procedural principle that is founded on eschewing the validity of imposing such convictions upon others?

If Robertson's recent revelation on the meaning of reproduction may be dismissed as a methodological aberration, then given the procedural premises of procreative liberty there is no compelling reason, other than harming persons, why cloning should be prohibited. It is a noncoital method of reproduction, entailing no greater range of collaboration than what is currently practiced. Although a decision to clone may seem repugnant, the very rationale of procreative liberty is to ensure respect for unpopular reproductive choices. Moreover, it secures an outcome similar to what is achieved by quality-control techniques.

In looking briefly now at four scenarios, we may spell out why human cloning would indeed be permissible within a secular framework of procreative liberty.

1. Individuals should have the right to clone themselves.

Although many people may judge this to be narcissistic, this does not mean that such a choice should not be respected by others. Nor would every decision to clone oneself be necessarily motivated by selfish intentions. For a sterile man, for instance, cloning would provide the only means of producing a biologically related son. Moreover, cloning oneself would not harm anyone, for one's clone cannot be harmed until he is alive. Nor is there necessarily any inherent indignity involved in replicating one's genotype, for cloning oneself is little more than creating a latter-day twin. If one has a fundamental right to pursue reproduction, then presumably one also has the right to reproduce oneself.

2. Individuals should have the right to attain desirable children.

Cloning could provide relatively easy and reliable access to the benefits of collaborative reproduction and quality-control measures. Prospective clients, for instance, might employ the services of a clinic owning a range of embryonic clones. Clients would watch videotapes or observe the living twins of these cloned embryos. Upon choosing a desirable child, clients would arrange an appropriate gestation process. Cloning could provide desirable children for individuals wishing to forgo the relatively lengthy and cumbersome process of managing various collaborative and quality-control techniques in favor of a package deal.

3. Individuals should have the right to attain a replacement child.

There are few experiences more tragic than the death of one's child. Although the clone would not be the same person as the dead child, the genetic replica could provide a source of comfort, ameliorating the suffering of grieving parents. This would be particularly true in the death of an only child when a parent had subsequently become infertile. Moreover, the desire to clone one's dead child is not necessarily worse than other motives, nor would the child's replacement status necessarily prove any more burdensome than other parental expectations.

4. Parents should have the right to clone their children in cases of dire medical necessity.

Suppose that one's daughter is suffering a fatal form of blood cancer. Her only hope for surviving is a bone marrow transplant, but no suitable donor can be found. Her clone would provide a perfectly compatible donor, thus saving her life. The parental desire here is similar to that of attaining a replacement child, with the additional altruistic motive of providing a life-saving medical resource. Moreover, there is no reason to believe that the latter-day twin would be any less loved or cared-for than her older sister.

As these scenarios illustrate, there is nothing inherent within Robertson's framework of procreative liberty prohibiting the cloning of humans. Since harm cannot be demonstrated, there is no compelling reason this option should be withheld from individuals exercising their reproductive rights. The procedural character of procreative liberty does not allow inserting a normative value on the "meaning" of reproduction in response to the development of a new technology. Robertson's own principle fails him precisely at the point where he wishes to make a comprehensive claim about the purpose of procreation, but ultimately he can do nothing more than try to persuade individuals to refrain from cloning while respecting their decision should they choose to do so. This is why, if something like procreative liberty is becoming as pervasive as I think it is, it is only a matter of time until cloning becomes one reproductive option among many.

Yet Robertson's intuitive reaction against cloning is correct, and unless we naively hope that individuals will simply choose not to do it, then we need to look at the "meaning" of reproduction within a normative rather than procedural framework. The problem with procreative liberty is its presumption that a child is an outcome of reproductive choices. As an alternative, I suggest we think about children as the culmination of a complex and purposeful process, and that procreation itself be viewed as a teleologically ordered pattern of practices. Children, then, are more the outgrowth of a relationship than the outcome of individual decisions. Consequently, the primary moral task is to assess to what extent the means of attaining children accord with or deviate from a normative ordering of procreation. In short, a framework of familial integrity rather than procreative liberty would give us a different reading of what is at stake in the prospect of human cloning. Before offering such an alternative reading, however, I will sketch out the rough contours of what I am calling familial integrity.

A Framework of Familial Integrity

The family involves the ordering of natural and social affinity. Ideally this entails a genetically unrelated wife and husband producing offspring who are genetically related to each other and to both of their parents. It is this ordering of natural and social affinity which gives procreation its full meaning; collapsing either dimension deprives the roles of spouse, parent, child, and sibling of their complete and mutual significance. The family also provides a place of unconditional belonging. Children are not routinely interviewed and invited to join a family, nor are they acquired as an accoutrement adorning an already established relationship. Rather, they grow out of an enlarging relationship to which they in turn contribute in establishing a family. In this respect, children are more properly given and received than they are sought and attained. A family comes into being, not as a result of reproductive acts or decisions, but through a movement of being opened up in providing a place of belonging.

We may say, then, that the family is characterized by an unfolding and enfolding of familial love. From the one-flesh unity of a wife and husband there unfolds an openness to the begetting rather than the making of children.[8] A couple is drawn toward being with children and together becoming a family. Indeed, a family cannot properly order its natural and social affinity, nor provide an adequate place of unconditional belonging, without a larger familial identity shaping the individuals and relationships comprising it. For a family is not simply a collection of spousal, parental, filial, and fraternal relationships, but a defining and delimiting reality in its own right. And without an unfolding and enfolding familial love, the family tends to become a compilation of cohabiting individuals held together either by unequal dependency, temporary necessity, or mutual agreement. This is why collaborative reproduction is disquieting, because it tends to reduce the family to a parental attainment of children rather than the embodiment of an unfolding and transforming love originating in the shared being of spouses, which is then opened up, drawn toward, and enfolded within a greater familial love.

With this framework of familial integrity in mind, the prospect of cloning humans should be greeted with grave wariness, for it distorts the ordering of natural and social affinity afforded by the family, thereby weakening its ability to provide a place of unconditional belonging, as well as marking a form of love which turns in upon itself rather than one being opened up and drawn out. These objections may be clarified by revisiting the scenarios used previously to justify the use of human cloning.

1. Individuals should not clone themselves because doing so disfigures the ordering of natural and social affinity afforded by the family.

I have tried to imagine what it would be like to clone myself. Presumably, I would use this technology to attain a child, satisfying a parental desire. Yet following his birth, whom would I behold? This question is prompted not so much by the confusion entailed in trying to determine whether this new being is my son, brother, or both, but rather, because, given this method of reproduction, these differentiated roles cannot emerge and develop. The enriching range of relationships devolving from a pluriformity of sexes and genetic endowments in which a new child has two parents is lost in favor of a uniformity of natural and social affinity. I am not saying I could not love or care for my clone. I think I could. I simply do not know how our relationship could be defined within the context of a family. We would both be deprived of a full sense of familial relatedness and belonging. For it is the distinctive character of the spousal, parental, filial, and sibling relationships which shapes the ordering of a family's natural and social affinity. Cloning oneself could only distort the distinctive, though integrally related, familial roles by negating the boundaries separating and delimiting the roles of parent, child, and sibling.

2. Attaining clones of desirable children is incompatible with the family as a place of unconditional belonging.

The family is built upon the one-flesh unity of a wife and husband, who out of the totality of their shared being bring into life a new being who is part of them and yet who is also wholly other than them. It is in the space circumscribed by this bond and disaffection that their mutual belonging is provided. It is within the unfolding spousal and parental forms of love into an enfolding familial love that parents and children come to belong with each other. This place of unconditional belonging, then, is bounded by the proper ordering of choice and chance: We may choose our mates, when to have children and how many to have, but we cannot choose the precise qualities of our children, nor our parents or the family in which we are given our belonging. In coming to see children as the outcome of reproductive decisions the family is debased to a means of satisfying parental desires, so that belonging becomes conditional upon the desirability of offspring whom parents choose to admit into their sphere of affection and attention. In this respect, selecting a desirable clone simply magnifies the most disturbing aspects of quality-control measures and collaborative reproduction, for it attempts to further subsume the element of chance into that of choice. For unlike quality-control measures and collaborative reproduction, which produce a unique genome and therefore an element of risk, cloning assures a specific genotype. Rather than enabling the family to be a place of unconditional belonging, cloning would only reinforce a further constriction in which conditional belonging is offered within an increasingly narrowing opening.

3. Cloning a replacement child violates the character of an unfolding and enfolding familial love.

Familial love is vulnerable. An expansive and unfolding love is accompanied by unexpected joy and happiness, and also unanticipated sorrow, suffering, and loss. These qualities are inseparable if the family is to provide an unconditional place of belonging. Hence parenthood is always accompanied by the twin elements of hope and risk. Attempting to replace a dead child with a clone, say, is to turn familial love in upon itself, for it tries to reach back and recapture what has been lost. Yet an unfolding familial love embraces the pain and suffering of its members, making them a part of its ongoing and enfolding life. No member of a family can truly be replaced, for a family is not simply a structure built with interchangeable parts, but a symbiotic affinity in its own unique right. If grieving parents should decide to have another child, this should not be a vain attempt to replace what has been lost, but a fitting compliance to an unfolding and enfolding familial love which is always accompanied by hope and risk.

4. Cloning one's child for the purpose of dire medical necessity is potentially the most justifiable scenario.

What follows, then, is not so much an absolute objection as a disquieting reservation. It would be fruitless to impugn a parental motive in this case as a desperate attempt to hold on to a dying child, or to argue that this latter-day twin would be any less loved or cherished. Cloning an ill child to secure bone marrow, for instance, may very well express a genuine parental love for a child who will otherwise die. Yet despite the sincerity of this motive, a cloud would nonetheless hang over the birth of a cloned child. This child would embody the undeniable fact that the primary purpose, perhaps even the sole reason, she was brought into being was to ensure the survival of her older sister. No matter how much love and affection she is given, no matter how much her inherent sense of dignity and self-worth is reinforced, the family would nevertheless have to deal with the reality that this latter-day twin's belonging in the family was conditioned upon the value of her particular collection of genes. As mentioned earlier, I do not know if this disquieting reservation is sufficient to prohibit cloning one's child for the purpose of dire medical necessity, but it should be at least sufficiently troubling to prompt serious deliberation well before the technology is in place to attempt it.

Conclusions

I have tried to demonstrate that evaluating the prospect of human cloning within the framework of familial integrity, as opposed to procreative liberty, gives us a different reading of what is at stake. In general, the cloning of humans should not be attempted because it disrupts the ordering of the family's natural and social affinity, distorts the family as a place of unconditional belonging, and violates the character of an unfolding and enfolding familial love. In this respect, I agree with Robertson's objection that cloning breaches the "meaning" of reproduction, and therefore should not be pursued.

Unlike Robertson, however, I have placed the "meaning" of human reproduction within a normative context of the family, a step he is unwilling to take. For to do so would require dismantling the individualistic presumptions underlying procreative liberty. Yet, as I have also tried to demonstrate, his objections are not sufficient to trump the rights of individuals from cloning themselves, their offspring, or other desirable children. To try to introduce a normative objection other than the avoidance of harm at the point of cloning is simply too late in the game. Rather, introducing a normative account of the "meaning" of human reproduction must take place early on, challenging such current practices as collaborative reproduction and quality control, if it is to influence so-called reproductive decisions.

It may be argued that my account of familial integrity is simply an attempt to impose an antiquated "inheritance myth,"[9] or that my objections to cloning in particular and reproductive technology in general reflect a slavish devotion to an outdated biology and to unwarranted fear that technology is destroying the meaning of human reproduction. Like it or not, with the advent of reproductive technology we have crossed a line from which there is no turning back. Something like procreative liberty must guide us in exercising greater control over the creation of our progeny. We will simply have to learn to choose wisely among our growing array of reproductive options, including the prospect of cloning.

Yet such an objection fails to recognize that no such line has been crossed. The so-called reproductive revolution is merely another attempt at asserting the Enlightenment's myth of the human mastery of nature. Rather than ordering procreative practices within a normative familial context, which takes into account delimiting and defining natural qualities, the family is instead distorted into an outcome of reproductive decisions. Consequently, the means of attaining children are not morally significant so long as no one is harmed in the choices that one makes.

Yet imposing this myth upon procreation destroys the very genius afforded by the family in the ordering of human life. This may be spelled out by looking briefly at adoption. Given my account of familial integrity, can an adoptive family embody the ordering of natural and social affinity, provide an unconditional place of belonging, and display an unfolding and enfolding of familial love as afforded by the one-flesh unity of marriage? It cannot if we believe that adoption is but one means among many of attaining children. Adoption, however, is an act of charity (*caritas*), responding to unfortunate circumstances in which parents are unable or unwilling to care for their children. Unlike surrogacy or gamete donation, a child is not brought into being for the purpose of being raised by individuals other than the child's natural parents. Hence, as Oliver O'Donovan has observed, "the biological parents will never cease to be the child's parents in a certain sense" and their "replacement is occasioned only by their own incapacity to fulfill their role. They do not act for adoptive parents; adoptive parents act for them."[10] Adoptive parents step in to take the place of persons unable to discharge their parental responsibilities, and in doing so they and their adopted child come to share a mutual belonging. This is why adoption is not restricted to infertile couples, for it involves extending familial hospitality to children who would not otherwise have a place of belonging. As an act of charity, adoption upholds familial integrity as an ordering of affinity within a pattern of unfolding and enfolding love without unduly denigrating or exalting either the natural or social dimensions of parenthood.

When adoption is invoked as a means of attaining children, implying that biological relatedness is thereby irrelevant, then by extension virtually any reproductive option becomes permissible so long as procedural safeguards are followed. Contrary to the belief that reproductive technology is driven by a so-called inheritance myth, it is motivated by a desire to control reproduction through the sheer force of human will. For if the genetic relation between children and parents is irrelevant, then it may range from none at all to, in the future, an exact replica of one progenitor. And in the absence of a normative account of procreation and the family, there is no standard to judge the morality of these choices other than avoiding harm. Yet this is to void procreation of its meaning, namely creation for the sake of some larger purpose beyond parental desires. In this respect, cloning is an exquisite parody of the one-flesh foundation of procreation, for it is one more step in reducing its purpose to whatever we will or choose it to be.

It is my hope that the specter of human cloning will prompt us to reappraise how we are coming to think about procreation, and that we will see cloning not as a novel and isolated technological development but continuous with a much larger program. My concern is not so much intervening into procreation per se, but rather the purposes for which these technologies are employed. For in the absence of a normative account of the family, I am afraid that parenthood may be reduced to a form of self-fulfillment through managed breeding, cut off from a normative ordering of natural and social affinity which prevents it from being subsumed into the equally destructive myths of inheritance or disembodied will. At the very least, I hope that invoking something like familial integrity might, in the ensuing debates over human cloning, keep the onus squarely on justifying its use rather than its prohibition.

I wish to express my gratitude to Oliver O'Donovan for his critical comments on an earlier draft of this chapter.

NOTES

1. See John Robertson, *Children of Choice: Freedom and the New Reproductive Technologies* (Princeton N.J.: Princeton University Press, 1994).
2. Ibid., 24.

3. Ibid., 119–45.
4. Ibid ., 167–70.
5. Ibid., 169.
6. Ibid.
7. Ibid.
8. See Paul Ramsey, *One Flesh: A Christian View of Sex Within, Outside and Before Marriage* (Bramcote, U.K.: Grove Books, 1975), and Oliver O'Donovan, *Begotten or Made?* (Oxford: Oxford University Press, 1984).
9. See, e.g., Ted Peters, *For the Love of Children: Genetic Technology and the Future of the Family* (Louisville, Ky.: Westminster John Knox Press, 1996), 19–30.
10. O'Donovan, *Begotten or Made?,* 37; see also 35–38.

10

The Brave New World of Cloning

A Christian Worldview Perspective

R. ALBERT MOHLER, JR.

"I WAS CONVINCED
that there was still plenty of time."[1] With those words the author
Aldous Huxley looked back to 1931 and the publication of his famous novel *Brave New World*. Huxley's vision of an oppressive
culture of total authoritarian control and social engineering was
among the most shocking literary events of the twentieth century.
But just twenty-seven years after the publication of *Brave New
World*, Huxley was already aware of his underestimation of the
threat represented by modern technocratic society.

News that scientists have cloned an adult sheep from nonre-
productive cells has shaken the scientific community and has set
loose an earthquake of concern in the larger culture. This report had
barely begun to sink into our cultural consciousness when further
reports of the cloning of monkeys from embryo cells and attempts
at human cloning raised the sense of ethical crisis.

The simple fact that an adult sheep had been produced through
cloning was a graphic indication of the remarkable advances
made in the field of genetics in recent years. The proposed use of
the cloned sheep and the impetus behind the experiment is pharmaceutical research, but this limited purpose only hints at the
countless purposes to which the technology can be directed.
Dolly, as the sheep is known, is the face of the future as the technology of cloning is advanced and applied.

The Cloning of Animals and the Ethics of Dominion

According to the Bible, human beings are granted and assigned
a dual responsibility by the Creator: dominion and stewardship. Human beings, made in the image of God, are to exercise dominion

and rule over the fish of the sea and over the birds of the sky and over the cattle and over all the earth, and over every creeping thing that creeps on the earth (Gen.1:28, NASB). This extensive rule sets the human being apart from the rest of creation and from the other creatures.

This rulership is translated into the intentional use of animals for human ends and the elevation of human needs and purposes above all other creatures. However, the dominion granted to human beings is not inherently ours; it is a delegated rulership. We rule over the animals by the authority of our Creator, and thus we will answer for our stewardship of our dominion.

What does this suggest about the issue of cloned animals? First, the acknowledgment of our delegated dominion should make clear that our rulership is limited. We are not to take the authority of the Creator as our own. Second, this principle of a delegated rulership should serve as a warning concerning the increasing artificiality of animal life at human hands. The increasing use of unnatural means of reproduction leads automatically to a sense of engineered life forms as human creations.

Put bluntly, we were not commanded or authorized to create new forms of life as extensions of our own designs and egos. Nightmarish scenarios of unforeseen consequences are easily imaginable. Further, the issue of cloned mammals threatens the biodiversity God clearly intended as a mark of God's creation. Cloned animals repeat the genetic code of the host animals, avoiding the genetic mixing that comes by natural reproduction. Performed on a wide scale, this could threaten to harm species or even threaten their survival from disease.

Without question, the development of cloning may provide advances in therapeutic technologies which will benefit human beings as well as animals. Nevertheless, the technology of cloning also raises the specter of transgenic animals—crossing species and creating customized new animal forms. Here again, the Christian worldview warns us that our stewardship and dominion of other creatures is to be exercised within limits imposed by the Creator. Many arguments on behalf of human "co-creation" with God are not biblically sustainable, and they indicate creaturely over-reaching and hubris. Human beings are assigned responsibility for the care, use, and enjoyment of animal creatures, but we are not granted license for their mechanistic manipulation, transgenic innovation, or ruthless violation.

One need not accept the ideology of the animal rights movement in order to question the moral character of these new technologies which threaten the integrity of animal life. We need not make abstract claims for the integrity of animal life. The distinction between human beings and the other living beings is central to the biblical text. Spiritual value is assigned to human life in a sense that is totally foreign and alien to animal life. Animal life is certainly not without value, as attested by the Creator's verdict on the goodness of animal creation. But animal life cannot be assigned the highest value, for such would be an inversion of the biblical hierarchy of value and moral responsibility.

The Cloning of Humans and the Reproductive Revolution

Though the cloning of a sheep was the proof that mammalian cloning could be achieved, few thoughtful persons could keep their minds on the lamb. The cloning of human beings—long limited to the domain of science fiction—now appeared to be an impending possibility. Ian Wilmut accepted the fact that cloning humans would be possible. "There is no reason in principle why you couldn't do it," he acknowledged. Yet he added, "All of us would find that offensive." [2]

Though his first statement remains to be demonstrated, his second statement is blatantly false. It is simply not true that all of us would find the cloning of human beings to be offensive. Indeed, an editorial published in *Nature* advised that human cloning "is likely to be achievable any time from one to ten years from now. Ethical constraints aside, there are even some rare genetic and medical disorders for which it would be a desirable way for a couple to produce offspring."[3] Bioethicist John Robertson agrees, adding that the cloning of a dying child or infertile adults might be morally justified.[4] Others, such as John

Fletcher, a former ethicist for the National Institutes of Health, assert that the cloning of a baby designed to provide a tissue-matched organ or bone marrow could also be justified. "The reasons for opposing this are not easy to argue," Fletcher commented.[5]

This is an issue of immediate, urgent, and universal importance. The cloning of a human being represents a radical break with the human past and with the established patterns of human life. The very possibility of human cloning is repulsive to many persons. Harvard neurobiologist Lisa Geller, who admitted that she could make no ethical distinction between in vitro fertilization and cloning, nevertheless confessed: "I admit it makes my stomach feel nervous." [6] The genetic revolution is perhaps the greatest ethical challenge of the new millennium—and that nervous stomach to which Geller admitted is about all the secular worldview can offer in response to this issue. Having denied the existence and authority of God the Creator, all that remains for modern secularists is the artificial morality of an ad hoc ethic. Any opposition to cloning—human or otherwise—is merely arbitrary. *Business Week* was positively ecstatic about the possibilities of cloning, and stated editorially: "The world should embrace the biological revolution, not cringe from it."[7] Yet, incongruous though it may seem, the same editorial warned: "There is no question that the notion of individuals cloning themselves is not only repugnant but also raises important questions." The possible development of human cloning raises a host of ethical quandaries. Who would be the "parents" of a cloned child? In an age of patented forms of life, could a cloned being be "owned," at least in genetic pattern? Will parents seek to clone children in order to provide tissues, organs, or bone marrow for transplant into another child? The secular worldview provides only tentative and provisional answers. I will argue that the Christian worldview alone can provide us with an ethical context and authority adequate to this task.

In the Image of God:
Human Beings and the Purpose of God

The biblical creation account presents the creation of human beings as the pinnacle of God's creative purpose. After creating the world and filling it with living creatures, God purposed to create human beings. The human creature, set apart from all other creatures, would bear the *imago dei*, the image of God. While the exact nature of the image of God in the human creature is not identified in detail, it clearly represents the spiritual character and capacity God established in us, and it sets the human creature apart from all other living beings. Though historic Christian theology holds that the *imago dei* has been corrupted by sin, it has not been obliterated, and thus the distinction between humanity and the animals remains. As Martin Luther explained: "Thus even if this image has been almost completely lost, there is still a great difference between the human being and the rest of the animals."[8]

Though the image of God in human beings has been corrupted by sin, it has not been removed, and this image is an essential mark of true humanity. Each human being is a special creation of God, made in God's own image. Human beings share certain common characteristics and features as well as a common form with specializations, but each person is unique by the design of the Creator. The status of human beings as created beings, each unique but all bearing the image of God, establishes a foundation for theological understanding.

The fact that the precise character of the image of God in humanity is unknown to us does not mean that we have no general knowledge of its meaning. The Reformed tradition has identified knowledge, righteousness, and holiness as a triad of qualities representing the image of God.[9] Each of these qualities establishes the human as qualitatively distinct from other creatures. Thomas Aquinas, the great synthesizer of the medieval tradition, defined the image of God as a function and capacity of human consciousness or intellect. This capacity exists in three stages, argued Thomas, rising from the potential knowledge of God, to the actual knowledge of God, to the perfect knowledge of God. John Calvin tied the concept of the image of God to the human capacity to glorify God, but accepted that every part of the human being is marked in some sense by the image of God, even though it is corrupted by sin. Herman Bavinck stated the issue clearly: "Man does not simply bear or have the image of God; he is the image of God."[10]

The biblical view of human value is rooted in the revealed

knowledge that we are made in God's image and thus that we are image-bearers by our very nature. Bavinck's reminder that this is essential to true humanity is echoed by Anthony Hoekema's insistence that the concept of the image of God is the "most distinctive feature of the biblical understanding of man."[11] Without the knowledge of the divine image, we do not know ourselves for what we are.

This makes clear the decisive distinction between the biblical and secular conceptions of human nature and value. The naturalistic understanding of humanity central to modernity accepts no theistic referent of value. Human beings are cosmic accidents, the fortuitous by-products of blind evolutionary process. As James Watson reflected, he came early to accept Linus Pauling's simple statement, "We came from chemistry."[12] Any value thus ascribed to human life is arbitrary, tentative, and necessarily self-referential. This explains why contemporary secular debates concerning the value or sanctity of human life are so inherently confused. We will ascribe value to ourselves by an act of the will. But as the murderous twentieth century has shown, those who ascribe value to human life by an act of the will can also deny that same value by a similar act of the will.

According to the biblical revelation, human beings, like all of creation, were created in order to glorify God. But human beings were created with a distinct and unique capacity to know, reverence, worship, and glorify the Creator. God made human beings, male and female, of his own good pleasure, in his own image, and to his own sovereign purpose. Thus, human beings are not mere biological artifacts or accidental forms of life. The special, purposeful, and direct creation of every human being in the image of God is central to the Christian worldview. Modernity's rejection and refutation of that revealed knowledge has set the stage for the rise of abortion, euthanasia, genetic manipulation, infanticide, and even genocide, all in the name of social responsibility and personal autonomy.

Genetic Manipulation and the Eugenic Temptation

As Daniel Kevles notes, the desire to breed better humans goes back as far as Plato, though Plato had no conception that genetic knowledge would one day put that goal within human reach.[13] Francis Galton's term eugenics (literally, "good in birth") is now a part of our cultural vocabulary, and the eugenic reality is a pressing cultural crisis.

The temptation to think of human breeding in eugenic terms is powerful and, in one sense, virtually unavoidable. No thoughtful person would suggest or recommend casual disregard of genetic knowledge regarding, for example, inherited genetic disorders such as Tay-Sachs disease. But the advent of genetic testing and the exploding knowledge of the human genome present entirely new eugenic opportunities and ethical challenges.

The crusades of the early eugenicists were directed at limiting the reproduction of those persons or races considered "inferior" and the enhancement of the human species by the intentional breeding of those considered racially or individually "superior." Eugenic experiments, movements, and theories were common in the early twentieth century in both Europe and the United States, and these often were presented as essentially hygienic and progressive in purpose.

The Human Genome Project represents the Manhattan Project of human genetics, and it will present humanity with the greatest ethical challenges of the coming century. Though this is seldom articulated or acknowledged in public, genetic testing currently available is used by some parents to decide if a developing fetus is worthy of life.

The ethical challenge of the genetic project is openly accepted by many scientists, including James Watson, who admitted that "the Nazis used leading members of the German human genetics and psychiatry communities to justify their genocide programs, first against the mentally ill and then the Jews and the Gypsies. We need no more vivid reminders that science in the wrong hands can do incalculable harm."[14] Of course, Watson is convinced that his hands are "right hands" and contemporary geneticists deny any goals of racial superiority. Nevertheless, the eugenic temptations of the present are every much as ominous as those of the past, and potentially far more threatening, for the new knowledge that was unavailable to the Nazi scientists is quickly setting the medical agenda. As Diane

B. Paul suggests, "over every contemporary discussion of eugenics falls the shadow of the Third Reich."[15]

The new eugenics is not driven by legal coercion but by something more like consumer choice. Parents, putting themselves in a consumer posture, are demanding increased genetic knowledge in order to give birth to designer babies, complete with chosen eye color, gender, and anticipated dispositions toward athletics, intellectual pursuits, or other chosen qualities or attributes. Needless to say, these parents also demand that their fetus be free from identifiable genetic flaws or diseases. As John A. Robertson admits, the focus on "offspring quality" changes the very nature of human reproduction. Every pregnancy becomes "tentative" until genetic screens indicate that the fetus is acceptable. This scenario is not an anticipation of future possibilities in genetic medicine, but a realization of present realities. If the fetus is judged to be of insufficient quality, it can be legally aborted at virtually any stage.

Robertson advocates this freedom under his proposed moral and legal principle of "procreative liberty."[16] As he argues, this libertarian principle can be applied to any reproductive situation, and state interference is nonexistent. Under the banner of "procreative liberty" we are free to employ any technology available in order to determine the quality of offspring desired. Those fetuses considered unfit are merely aborted without moral consequence or consideration.

In response to such suggestions, Philip Kitcher argues that having "left the garden of genetic innocence, some form of eugenics is inescapable, and our first task must be to discover where among the available options we can find the safest home."[17] Kitcher calls for the development of "utopian eugenics" based on the most sophisticated genetic testing, and argues for the genetic enhancement of the human species as a social responsibility.

The moral consequences of this would be dramatic indeed. Cloning would make possible the eventual desexualization of the human race and would allow eugenicists to transcend the "breeding" issues of the early eugenic movements. The new eugenic vision could avoid sexual reproduction altogether and, employing much the same technologies as used to "create" transgenic animals, could modify the genetic structure of the embryo so as to customize and determine virtually every genetic trait. Thus, the cloning of human beings would allow a dramatic and radical extension of the eugenic vision by allowing for the direct genetic customization of the embryo and the mass asexual production of identical embryos. Such a vision brings to mind the busy hatcheries of Huxley's *Brave New World* and the antiseptic sterility of his nightmare of totalitarian control.

Those who claim that the new eugenics will be free from all coercion are either hopelessly naive or deliberately disingenuous. Anyone familiar with the economic dynamics behind so many supposed medical decisions will know that coercion is already a reality. Pressure is brought on many parents to abort a fetus likely to require expensive medical attention. This pressure already exists as a form of coercion, but it is likely to be only a hint of what is to come. Social pressure, if not social policy, will reward those who allow or encourage eugenic decisions.

Furthermore, while "consumer" eugenics may be free from state coercion or open racial discrimination, it clearly aims at the birth of babies free from all unwanted or undesirable genetic traits and possessing those traits chosen as desirable. Philip Kitcher argues that as genetic counseling becomes generally available, a form of laissez-faire eugenics inevitably results. This laissez-faire eugenics is not, however, as free from discrimination and coercion as its proponents may claim.

Most fundamentally, the eugenicist vision represents our human attempt to define ourselves and our destiny. By unlocking the genetic code, by laying naked the genome, we will become masters of our own destiny. As human beings, we will define ourselves, improve ourselves, customize ourselves, replicate ourselves, and, in the final act of hubris, redeem ourselves through our genetically enhanced and clonally produced progeny.

Artificial Reproduction and
the Destruction of the Family

Sociobiologists explain the emergence and survival of the family in terms of evolutionary development and the need for a stable breeding unit. Given the present stage of human development, the family is passing as a necessity, and contemporary persons are re-defining relationships to serve other, more individualized needs. Modernity, with its focus on autonomous individualism and liberation from traditional structures, represents a threatening environment for the family unit. The sexual revolution has severed the link between sexual fidelity and marital integrity. Modern contraceptives have allowed unlimited sex without procreative consequences, and the family has been dethroned from its exalted status and stripped of its functions.

Modern feminism has targeted the family as a domestic prison from which women should make a clean escape, and motherhood is seen as a biological imposition. The homosexual movement has sought to redefine the family by demanding acceptance and recognition of same-sex partnerships, and both male and female same-sex couples claim the right to children, if not progeny. Increasing numbers of unmarried women now become pregnant through donor insemination or other reproductive technologies, and lesbian groups have even established fertilization centers and support groups. Clearly, the traditional heterosexual nuclear family is no longer considered the only culturally approved unit of human reproduction.

The possibility of human cloning allows for the final emancipation of human reproduction from the marital relationship. Indeed, cloning would allow for the emancipation of human reproduction from any relationship. Because cloning removes the need for either sperm or egg, no "parent" is necessary. At this point, however, a womb is still necessary for implantation and gestation. Put bluntly, women would be needed as available wombs, if not as biological mothers. Cell biologist Ursula Goodenough of Washington University stated the obvious corollary: "There'd be no need for men."[18] Modernity's assault on the family would thus be complete with the development of cloning. Already stripped of its social functions, the family would now be rendered biologically unnecessary, if not irrelevant. Final liberation from the family and the conjugal bond would be achieved.

Modern secularism may celebrate this emancipation as human progress as our species leaves the vestiges of the premodern era behind. But the Christian worldview refutes this secular illusion. As defined by biblical revelation, the family is neither the accidental by-product of social evolution nor merely the convenient boundary for socially sanctioned sexual relationships. According to Scripture, the family is God's gracious gift for our protection, our sexual integrity, and our enjoyment. The conjugal bond is not a biological trap from which we should seek escape. The marital relationship is the only divinely sanctioned locus of human sexuality and the bearing of children. The blessing of children is the intended result of the marital bond and the conjugal act.

Surrogate motherhood, artificial insemination, and in vitro fertilization already separate fertility and child bearing from the conjugal act, and, in many cases, from the marital relationship. This is a separation of great moral consequence. As Gilbert Meilaender has commented, "In our world there are countless ways to 'have' a child, but the fact that the end 'product' is the same does not mean that we have done the same thing." [19]

Moral philosophers such as Leon Kass and Oliver O'Donovan have noted that our language betrays a shift in consciousness. O'Donovan, Regius Professor of Moral and Pastoral Theology at Oxford University, reminds us that the Nicene Creed affirms that Jesus Christ, the only Son of the Father was, from eternity, "begotten not made." We, as human beings, are not in a position to "make" other humans, but only to beget them by God's intended design. As O'Donovan notes, "We have to consider the nature of this human begetting in a culture which has been overwhelmed by making—that is to say, in a technological culture."[20] The shift from "begetting" to "making" noted by O'Donovan reflects the technological worldview of the age. A similar pattern is noted by Leon Kass of the University of Chicago, who traces the shift from procreation to reproduction. Procreation, asserts Kass, reflects the acknowledgment of a Creator and the generative act of creation.

Reproduction, on the other hand, is a "metaphor of the factory."[21] The factory is precisely the image Huxley presented as the reproductive future, and this factory (or laboratory) is the explicit rejection of the marital relationship, the integrity of the family, and our identity as the creature rather than the Creator.

Resisting the Eugenic Temptation

Human cloning, along with other genetic technologies, represents the over-reaching of the creature. No longer satisfied with our creaturely status, we will become our own creators, the masters of our species and all others. As John Robertson admits, some now seek to take responsibility for a revolutionary transition in human nature in order to become "creators of ourselves."[22]

As early as 1968, a report of the National Academy of Sciences declared that the Copernican and Darwinian revolutions would now be followed by the power of modern man to "guide his own evolution."[23] Carl Sagan claimed that such a threshold had already been crossed and that "We are the first species to have taken evolution into our own hands." [24] The worldview of secular naturalism leads inevitably to such a conclusion. Mainstream evolutionary scientists argue against any design in the universe and any special value to human beings, other than the evolutionary development of consciousness. Given such a worldview, which denies both Creator and creation, the aspiration to become masters of our own destiny is natural and rational. If we are not created in the image of God, then we will be our own gods. If there is no divine Creator, no Maker of heaven and earth, then we will have to take creation into our own hands.

The eugenic temptation is so powerful that only the Christian worldview can restrain it. Scripture alone reveals our creaturely identity, our sinfulness, and the limits of our authority and responsibility. We are not the Creator, and the responsibility to assume control of the universe is not ours. God the Creator rules over all and has revealed his intention for us in laws and commandments that demand our obedience and in limitations that demand our respect.

We are not to play God. As the late Paul Ramsey argues: "We ought rather to live with charity amid the limits of a biological and historical existence which God created for the good and simple reason that, for all its corruption, it is now—and for the temporal future will be—the good realm in which man and his welfare are to be found and served." [25]

The very notion of moral limits is foreign to the secular mind. Increasingly, the worldviews of modern secularistic scientism and scriptural Christianity are understood to be incompatible and diametrically opposed. As a consequence, moral discourse on issues such as cloning is often grossly confused or totally absent. Faced with the potential development of human cloning, the modern secular worldview develops a queasy stomach, but will never be able to establish a moral conviction. Its ad hoc morality and arbitrary judgments will never lead to a common understanding, much less to a defense of the sanctity of life.

Over twenty-five years ago, James Watson declared the likely advent of "clonal man." Admitting that this development would be deeply upsetting to many persons, Watson raised the question, "Is this what we want?"[26] Watson, who was the first director of the Human Genome Project and has championed the rise of genetic knowledge and technologies, ended his essay by warning that "if we do not think about it now, the possibility of our having a free choice will one day suddenly be gone."[27]

That day may now be very close at hand. Christians should engage in this debate on biblical terms and contend for the sanctity of all created life as well as for the distinction between the creature and the Creator. All technologies, including modern genetics, must be evaluated in terms of the biblical revelation and the totality of the Christian worldview.

The troubling tangle of ethical issues involved in genetic technologies represents an urgent challenge to the Christian church as the people of the truth. The new technologies cannot be naively dismissed nor blissfully embraced. This generation of Christians must regain the disciplines of moral discernment and cultural engagement. The Brave New World is upon us.

NOTES

1. Aldous Huxley, *Brave New World Revisited* (New York: Harper and Row, 1958), 3.

2. Gina Kolata, "With Cloning of a Sheep, the Ethical Ground Shifts," *The New York Times*, February 24, 1997, A1.

3. "Caught Napping by Clones: Pleas for Ethical Advice on Mammalian Cloning Reveal a Lack of Foresight," *Nature* 385 (1997): 6619.

4. Kolata, "Ethical Ground Shifts."

5. Jeffrey Kluger, "Will We Follow the Sheep?" *Time*, March 10, 1997, 67–73, at 70.

6. Ibid.

7. "Don't Be Afraid of Genetic Research," *Business Week*, March 10, 1997, 126.

8. Martin Luther, Lectures on Genesis, Chapters 1–5, *Luther's Works*, vol. 1, ed. Jaroslav Pelikan (St. Louis: Concordia Publishing House, 1958), 67.

9. G. C. Berkouwer, *Man: The Image of God, Studies in Dogmatics*, trans. Dirk W. Jellema (Grand Rapids: Eerdmans, 1962), 88.

10. Cited in Anthony A. Hoekema, *Created in God's Image* (Grand Rapids: Eerdmans, 1986), 65.

11. Ibid., 11.

12. James D. Watson, "A Personal View of the Project," in *The Code of Codes: Scientific and Social Issues in the Human Genome Project*, ed. Daniel J. Kevles and Leroy Hood (Cambridge, Mass.: Harvard University Press, 1992), 164.

13. Daniel Kevles, "Out of Eugenics," in Kevles and Hood, 4.

14. Evelyn Fox Keller, "Nature, Nurture, and the Human Genome Project," in Kevles and Hood, 299.

15. Diane B. Paul, *Controlling Human Heredity: 1865 to the Present* (Atlantic Highlands, N.J.: Humanities Press, 1995), 134.

16. See John A. Robertson, *Children of Choice: Freedom and the New Reproductive Technologies* (Princeton, N.J.: Princeton University Press, 1994).

17. Philip Kitcher, *The Lives to Come: The Genetic Revolution and Human Possibilities* (New York: Simon and Schuster, 1996), 204.

18. Kolata, p. A–1.

19. Gilbert Meilaender, *Bioethics: A Primer for Christians* (Grand Rapids: Eerdmans, 1996), 15.

20. Oliver O Donovan, *Begotten or Made?* (Oxford: Oxford University Press, 1984), 2.

21. Cited in Meilaender, p. 11. See Leon Kass, *Toward a More Natural Science* (New York: The Free Press, 1985), 48.
22. Robertson, 274.
23. See Keller, 288.
24. Cited in Harold Varmus, "Genetics: The Ethical Problem with Knowledge," *Vital Speeches of the Day* (March 15, 1996), 337.
25. Paul Ramsey, *Fabricated Man: The Ethics of Genetic Control* (New Haven, Conn.: Yale University Press, 1970), 149.
26. James D. Watson, "Moving Toward the Clonal Man: Is This What We Want?" *Atlantic Monthly* 227 (May 1971): 50–53.
27. Ibid., 53.

11

Between Eden and Babel

ROGER L. SHINN

■■■ THE POSSIBLE ■■■■■■■■■■■■■■■■■■■
cloning of human beings brings together two compelling interests. It
is, first, an issue in its own right, alive with anxieties and conflicts
that reach into the mystery of selfhood. It is, second, a case study in
the interaction of an exploding science with moral concerns, politics,
and economics. For people of the historic religious communities it
raises again perennial issues of how they relate their convictions of
faith to public policies in modern pluralistic societies.

Five Propositions

I begin with five general propositions, none of which dictate
precise conclusions, but all of which bear upon personal and public decisions.

1. The issue, in its specificity, is new.

No law from Sinai, no command from a sacred Mount, nothing
in the Buddhist eightfold path or the Muslim sharia decrees: Thou
shalt or shalt not clone. The historic philosophers are equally
silent. We are engaged in exploratory ethics.

2. Scientific achievements force the new issues on our atten-
tion.

Four centuries ago Francis Bacon declared, "Knowledge is
power." It is not only power. The thrill of discovery and awe before beauty are part of the glory of science. But Bacon's insight is
more forceful today than ever. And the use of power is always an
ethical concern. The discovery of DNA in the nucleus of living
cells is as world-shaking as the discovery of explosive energy in

the nucleus of the atom. It may be even more disturbing because it reaches into the mysteries of human self-consciousness.

3. Science does not prescribe the uses of its powers.

Scientists cannot know, let alone control, the consequences of their discoveries. Some of the physicists who contributed to the development of nuclear energy soon objected to the use of nuclear weapons. They could not control the powers they unleashed. Nor should we wish that they could. Those who are affected for good or ill by scientific discoveries deserve a voice in their application. Scientists have the right and responsibility to participate in the uses of their knowledge and skills. But so do a lot of other people—above all, in a democratic society.

4. Wise ethical decisions require the active interaction of scientists with the wider public.

To ignore the expert knowledge and insight of scientists is to invite stupid or disastrous results. To turn over to those experts the ethical decisions of our time is to abdicate public responsibility. The possibility of wisdom comes in the interaction. We cannot simply separate roles, assigning to scientists the production of knowledge and to policy-makers its uses. That division of responsibilities is too glib. It neglects the ethical insights that come from scientists, and it neglects the need for others to interact energetically with scientific specialists. Scientists are not a neutral panel, who dispense answers to inquiring individuals and political actors. Scientific specialists must respond to questions that they, as scientists, do not ask. The knowledge produced by scientists often depends on their goals; and others, with different goals, may seek different evidence. Public policy comes out of the concerns of many groups—of poets, prophets, politicians, money-makers, and visionaries and realists from all walks of life—as these all face structures of nature and the social order.

5. Therefore it is important that everybody get in on the act.

That does not mean that everybody's opinion is equally valid. Some opinions are mistaken and some are harmful: those that seize upon scientific advances primarily to grab profits, to reinforce their own prejudices, or to dominate other nations. But decisions rightly take place in many arenas of life. Decisions about the uses of genetics, including cloning, will rise out of the beliefs and perceived interests of scientific specialists, family physicians, parents, business corporations, political authorities who appropriate money and pass laws, sports enthusiasts, social workers, and just about everybody else.

Cloning—Old and New

Cloning is an old, old story, primeval in its history. Dictionaries commonly define clones as organisms derived from other organisms and continuing the same genetic makeup. Some biologists prefer to narrow the term to cell propagation. Here I begin with the broad concept, then move to the more precise one.

All of us have experience with vegetative cloning. We may divide an African violet into two or three segments, then report them individually as genetically identical but obviously separate plants. There is no way to label parent and offspring in this democracy of equals. Or we may take cuttings from one plant and root them or graft them onto another rootstock to produce more plants. The millions of such a loved rose as Peace, though scattered around the world, are clones of the original hybrid—or, more often, clones of clones of clones of clones. Parents and offspring are all genetic replicas. New techniques, reproducing clones from single cells, may speed the reproduction of future hybrids.

All these processes involve asexual reproduction. Sexual reproduction is a far different story. It is the marvelous invention of nature—shall we say of God?—that enables two parents to beget offspring combining traits of both. The "children," whether of roses or of people, are unique. They embody both continuity with and change from the parents.

As important as sex is death. Plants that reproduce by cloning are more or less immortal. I say more or less, because no biological life persists forever. Biologists estimate that something like 95% of species of earth are extinct, and earth itself is not eternal.

But sexual reproduction goes with a life cycle, which we strain to extend but cannot revoke. As persons we lament death. For nature, it is a great idea, requiring old generations to give way to new. With cloning, while individual specimens die, the genetic identity persists, unconstrained by a predetermined life cycle.

Thus cloning, for all the radical novelty of its possible use, is essentially a conservative process: Its effect is to continue an unchanged identity. Sexual reproduction is the more radical process, providing for continuous innovation.

One practice, new to the present generation, is planned gene cloning. A familiar example is insulin. The hormone, extracted from the pancreas of sheep or cattle, is used to remedy human diabetes, caused by a deficiency of insulin. Now the human gene for insulin can be extracted from a person and planted in a bacterial cell where it multiplies by cloning and can then be injected into human patients.

There are other examples, some in practice and others projected. Cell cloning, once impossible and irrelevant to human beings, now has come to have a recognizable bearing on human life and health. However, all these developments have come rather quietly, with little public excitement or anxiety.

With the cloning of animals comes new excitement and new nervousness. Hopes and fears come closer to ourselves.

Still, the first steps were gradual and got little public attention. When tadpoles were cloned in 1952 and frogs in 1962, few people noticed. In 1981 mice were cloned from a seven-day-old embryo in Switzerland. Sheep and cow embryos were first cloned about ten years ago.

Then in a more startling experiment, as the press reports: "In 1993, embryologists at George Washington University cloned human embryos; they took cells from 17 human embryos (defective ones that an infertility clinic was going to discard), all two to eight cells in size. They teased apart the cells, grew each one in a lab dish and got a few 32-cell embryos—a size that could be implanted in a woman (though they weren't)."[1] Why did they stop? They were entering into experiments that aroused anxieties that have led to various restrictions, some legal, on experiments with fetal material.

Early Discussions about Human Cloning

In 1966–67 Joshua Lederberg of Stanford University, a Nobel laureate in biology, opened widespread discussions of human cloning. Although his several published statements stopped short of advocacy, they were often taken as recommendations. His motives were candidly eugenic: the improvement of the genetic qualities of humankind. Discussions of cloning erupted in colleges and professional societies. Lederberg persuaded few, but he provoked many responses. Theologian Paul Ramsey's reply in 1968 became a classic for those who opposed human cloning.[2]

Then the subject fell into neglect. Other scientific developments on genetic therapy and modification of the human germ line seemed more exciting. Lederberg thought that genetic manipulation would be impossible, because it required too minute a kind of surgery on human cells. With the discovery of "chemical scissors" or restriction enzymes, geneticists began to rearrange DNA within human cells. Cloning, I have already said, is basically conservative in its thrust, although it can have radical consequences. The manipulation of DNA, often called genetic engineering, is far more radical in its aim to modify, not simply continue, the genetic heritage of the past. In 1982 a President's Commission published a small but competent study, *Splicing Life*. It was a response to a request to President Carter from the General Secretaries of the National Council of Churches, the Synagogue Council of America, and the United States Catholic Conference. The book barely mentioned cloning in a footnote: "The technology to clone a human being does not—and may never—exist."[3] My book of 1996, *The New Genetics: Challenges for Science, Faith, and Politics*,[4] does not discuss cloning. The omission, though now surprising, was not a slip-up; I deliberately chose to focus on genetic therapies, where the action seemed to be.

I mention the early discussions because, given the short memory of the news media, the churches, and the public, it might seem that current discussions must start from ground zero. The *New York Times*, putting a headline on Gustav Niebuhr's report of religious responses to cloning (March 1, 1997), said that "suddenly" the churches were giving attention to the ethical quandaries of cloning. Current debaters might be wise to take account of past discussions rather than repeat them unknowingly.

The unexpected event was the cloning of a ewe and the birth of a lamb in Scotland, reported in early 1997. Dolly the lamb quickly became more famous than most of the leaders of nations around the world. At about the same time, experimentalists cloned rhesus monkeys in Oregon. Most people never heard about that. Since monkeys are more closely related to human beings than sheep, why did Dolly get the Oscar, the Tony, and the MVP award of the animal world? The answer lies in a signally important distinction. The monkeys were cloned from a fertilized egg; Dolly, from the body cells of an adult ewe.

An egg, when joined by a sperm, quickly begins dividing into two, then four, then eight cells, and so on. The initial divided cells are all alike. Then differentiation sets in. The cells, as they further subdivide, start the specialization that will make differing cells become parts of arms, legs, brains, eyes, ears, livers, intestines, and so on. In the amazing ways of life, each cell (excepting sperm, ova, and red corpuscles) has the genetic code for the complete person. But some of those genes are "turned on" ("expressed," biologists say) and others turned off. So we do not grow eyes on our elbows and hair on our hearts and toenails on our eyes. Experimentalists have grown fruit flies with eyes at odd places, but nobody has done this with people and nobody (I hope) ever will.

In the cloning of a fertilized egg, each undifferentiated cell has the potentiality of becoming a total frog or mouse or monkey. But after differentiation sets in, the cells are destined for special roles and lose the capacity to reproduce the total organism. Dr. Ian Wilmut, the Scottish embryologist, succeeded in making those specialized cells—of a ewe's udder—regress and reclaim their original capacity to produce a whole sheep. He did this by a careful process of semi-starvation of those cells. Then he took an egg from another ewe, removed its nucleus, introduced the cell from the udder, fused the two with a spark of electricity, let the new embryonic cell multiply, and implanted the embryo into a third ewe, the surrogate mother. One day a lamb, Dolly, was born.

That technical achievement had practical importance. The reason for cloning—if there is a reason—is to replicate an animal
with known characteristics. If you clone an embryonic cell, you
don't know whether that cell is any better (for your purposes) than
any other cell from the same parents. You have no practical advantage over the specialized breeding that is already popular. But
if you clone a cell from a mature animal, you can select the best
(again, for your purposes) of all candidates. So Dolly won the
celebrity that was denied to the rhesus monkeys.

Immediately human speculation went to work. Would we want
human cloning? Who would be our candidates? Michael Jordan
was a favorite. Why he? If anybody had proposed Bill Clinton or
Newt Gingrich—not to mention Boris Yeltsin or Saddam Hus-
sein—violent objections would erupt. Most of us don't know
much about Michael Jordan as a family man, personal friend,
politician, or artist; we know that he does his job well. In public
discussion Jordan and most of the examples were males, a sign of
gender bias. The smart riposte was that cloning had the possibility of making males unnecessary.

Beneath the mental fracases were some deep ethical questions.
Dolly had earned her fifteen-plus moments of fame. But profound
issues were with us for far longer.

The Ethics of Human Cloning

Is there any justification for human cloning? If so, what might
it be? Could it benefit various rival ethnic or national or ideological groups, the cloned persons, the human race?

The immediate responses were mostly, though not entirely,
negative. According to the press, Dr. Wilmut opposed human
cloning. "We can't see a clinical reason to copy a human being. In
this country it is illegal already. Furthermore, we are briefing authorities to make sure this technique is not misused. . . . We think
it would be ethically unacceptable and certainly would not want
to be involved in that project."[5] Others pointed out that cloning is
illegal in most European countries. The Director-General of the
World Health Organization, Hiroshi Nakajima, stated publicly:

"WHO considers the use of cloning for the replication of human individuals to be ethically unacceptable."[6]

President Clinton had earlier signed an executive order forbidding use of federal money to create embryos for research purposes. At that time he warned against "trying to play God." Now he added: "Each human life is unique, born of a miracle that reaches beyond laboratory science. I believe we must respect this profound gift and resist the temptation to replicate ourselves."[7] As some congressional leaders called for immediate legislation, Clinton asked for recommendations from the National Bioethics Advisory Commission. Its response in June 1997 proposed a legislative ban, initially of three to five years, on attempts to clone human beings. More important than its tentative judgment are the reasons that influence its opinions—and the opinions of us all. Certainly there is a wide, though not unanimous, public anxiety about human cloning. But public uneasiness often changes. People get used to practices—e.g., heart transplants—that once worried them. What considerations are likely to endure?

I begin with a contingent issue, utterly important now, but contingent because it may change. It is the issue of risk. The statistics of risk are foreboding. In the case of Dolly, Wilmut needed 277 attempts. Only 29 resulted in embryos that survived more than six days. These led to thirteen pregnancies. All miscarried, some with malformations, except Dolly.

Certainly our society will not tolerate treating human beings that way. Indeed, there is a major question whether we should treat sheep that way—an issue that has received scant attention in the public discussions.

What risks should we accept for the sake of presumed benefits? The old Kantian axiom is still impressive: We should never treat human beings solely as means and not as ends. In any society some of us are sometimes means to the ends of others, and all of us use others as means to our ends. But human dignity—"the image of God" in biblical language—means that people are always more than means. Medical ethics asks that people not be subjected to experiments without their "informed consent." There is no way to elicit informed consent from the experimental clone. Experimenters can truthfully reply that there is no risk-free life and no risk-free pregnancy. None of us gave informed consent to our own birth or genome. So what safeguards should we demand before human cloning? One answer would be that the risk should not be greater than in a normal pregnancy begun by a voluntary sexual relationship.

The issue of risk is utterly serious, but contingent because it will change. Many once-dangerous medical procedures have become routine. We may expect that technical progress will make cloning less risky—how much less we cannot now know. More fundamental issues are not likely to change because of technical achievements. We face age-old questions of what it is to be a person. How does this amazingly complicated conglomerate of protoplasm become a human self, and what respect or reverence is due to that person and the natural processes that produced it? The old-fashioned method of procreation has a lot going for it. That a child, a uniquely new person, should be born of the most intimate human love with a genetic legacy from loving parents is beautifully appropriate. That, of course, is not the blessing of all children. Some are born of lust, of rape, of careless indulgence—all of which may be less appropriate than cloning.

The question remains: Is there an unbearable arrogance in dictating the genome of a future individual and in moving from the processes of nature (for Christians, the divinely created order) to processes of manufacture in which manipulation replaces personal intimacy? The birth of Dolly evoked for many the question of William Blake, "Little lamb, who made thee?" Will future children answer that question, "A clinician made me in order to impose on me somebody else's genome"?

Are there really people so self-infatuated as to want to impose their own genetic identity on another? On the record, yes. The *New York Times Magazine* (May 28, 1997, p. 18) reported on one Randolfe Wicker, head of the Cloning Rights United Front in New York, who worried that "spineless politicians" would outlaw cloning: "I've already contacted a scientist rumored to be developing human cloning technology. My decision to clone myself should not be the Government's business or Cardinal O'Connor's. . . . Cloning is hugely significant. It's part of the reproductive rights of every human being." If that is said tongue-in-cheek, it shows a big tongue and a lot of cheek. It also shows total indifference to the interests of the infant to be cloned from a donor of notably unadmirable qualities.

Actually there may be less reason to worry about blatant ego-maniacs than about persons persuaded by admirers to do their duty to improve the human race. In the varieties of human societies there are despots and demagogues, would-be messiahs, scientists and athletes, entertainers and celebrities of infinite persuasions. The philosopher Nietzsche used to point out that every person is unique and unrepeatable in all history, a reality both wonderful and frightening. Although Nietzsche would not appreciate my saying so, he expressed a secularized echo of that awe for the uniqueness of persons that was first expressed by Jeremiah, who trusted that God called him before God formed him in his mother's womb, or by Jesus, who told us that our deeds for "the least of these" are our deeds for God.

The reality of identical twins is, of course, a fact of experience. They are clones, and they need not suffer embarrassment or loss of identity because of that fact. They are persons, each with an individual self-consciousness. Neither has the burden of knowing that s/he was manipulated into existence as an imitation or replication of a possessive parent.

The aim of replication is, in any case, doomed to failure. Resemblance, yes; replication, no. The individual arises out of the interaction of a genetic constitution with other persons and a culture. Imagine the birth four thousand years ago, in jungle or wilderness, of a person with genetic capacities comparable to Mozart's. The idea is not incredible; geneticists usually estimate that the genetic constitution of humanity has not improved in the past six or eight thousand years. But that person would not have composed symphonies or operas. Out of interaction of genetic capacity and society emerged the genius of Mozart, far different from any clone of the ancient past or of today. The cloned child is an identical twin with the older donor. The difference in age heightens the difference in identity. The moral problem of cloning is not that it will produce replicas; it is that the desire for replication is itself suspect and, yes, irreverent.

Think also of the burden imposed on those persons who know they were brought into existence to be genetic replicas of other people. The harm already done by parents trying to impose their expectations on children could be magnified many times. Given these considerations, both biblical and practical, I can imagine a person—in fact, myself—saying: "I don't want to be cloned. I prefer that my children have their fresh start in life rather than be imitations of me." (I quickly admit that I am experiencing no social pressure to be cloned.)

Some special reasons are proposed to justify cloning: to produce a child who could provide an organ transplant to an ailing sibling, or to perpetuate the existence of a terminally ill child. Such reasons either see the clone as a means to be employed by others or embody illusions about personal identity. More persistent is the desire to improve the human race—to multiply superlative athletes, great scientists, heroic soldiers, ambitious money-makers. Again, all the issues of eugenics, with its long history of prejudiced judgments, arise. We may claim that we can rise above those past errors, but that is exactly the time when we had better distrust ourselves.

Thus I conclude that I have not seen a reason that justifies human cloning. Some day I may possibly be shown a reason—perhaps the proposal for a cloning of fetal tissue for the sake of new knowledge, without the prospect of producing a new person. I will listen to any such reason with deep suspicion. Conceivably it may persuade me.

What next? It is one thing for a person like me to oppose cloning. But does that mean I want it forbidden? Most of us have many moral beliefs that we do not want imposed on others. Yet all legislation (except purely administrative regulations) rests on moral convictions. I repeat, cloning is forbidden by most European countries and discouraged by the World Health Organization. I think there is a sufficient public interest to justify a legal prohibition if a substantial body of belief supports it. The prohibition might resemble civil rights legislation: It is illegal to deny people certain defined rights because of their race or color. Society may decide that a person has the right not to be manufactured to the specifications of a parent, a sibling, or a laboratory experimenter.

Some are arguing that a prohibition of human cloning is useless, since somebody (or several somebodies) will always find a way to evade the law. Kirkpatrick Sale or his editor has put a headline over his article, "Ban Cloning? Not a Chance."[8] But laws against theft and murder are also evaded. That is no reason to abolish the laws.

Eden and Babel

Two biblical images hover over a Christian ethic of cloning, as over a Christian ethic of all technological power. In Eden the human creature is given "dominion" over the garden and a responsibility "to till and keep it" (Gen.1:26, 2:15). The dominion is not boundless. It does not extend to the Pleiades and Orion (Amos 5:8) or to the mountain goats, hawks, the crocodile and hippopotamus (Job 39–41). These are the reminders that this world was not created by us or for us. Yet within it we have a sacred responsibility.

The other image is that of Babel (Gen.11). Here ambition, the desire to be like God, combined with technological power brought historical chaos.

These two images do not prescribe the right uses of genetics in the work of caring for and healing the creation. They can guide us as we explore ethics for our time.

The New Testament reinforces these images. Even more than the Hebrew Bible, its expectation of a New Creation tells of the tentative nature of all planetary history. It nowhere suggests that scientific technology is the New Creator, even less that technology should seek to replicate old patterns rather than welcome the new. Christians cannot expect a pluralistic society to adopt an ethic based solely on Christian belief. They can declare their beliefs and seek to live by them. Doing that, they may discover that their ethical insights have some persuasiveness for humankind.

NOTES

1. Sharon Begley, "Little Lamb, Who Made Thee?" *Newsweek*, March 10, 1997, 54–55.
2. Paul Ramsey, "Shall We Clone a Man?" in *Fabricated Man* (New Haven, Conn.: Yale University Press, 1970). An address of 1968, first published in Kenneth Vaux, ed., *Who Shall Live? Medicine, Technology, Ethics* (Philadelphia: Fortress Press, 1970).
3. President's Commission for the Study of Ethical Problems in Medicine and Biomedical and Behavioral Research, *Splicing Life: The Social and Ethical Issues of Genetic Engineering with Human Beings* (Washington, D.C.: U.S. Government Printing Office, 1982), p. 10, n. 6.
4. Roger L. Shinn, *The New Genetics: Challenges for Science, Faith, and Politics* (Wakefield, R.I., and London: Moyer Bell, 1996).
5. *The New York Times*, February 24, 1997, B8. Associated Press dispatch, in *Waterbury Republican-American*, February 24, 1997, 1A.
6. Reported in the *Christian Century*, March 19–26, 1997.
7. Ibid., 286.
8. *The New York Times*, March 7, 1997, Op-Ed page.

12

At the Beginning

RONALD COLE-TURNER

███ MOST AMERICANS ███████████████████████
oppose reproductive human cloning.[1] Perhaps they imagine the
worst sorts of applications: cloned rock stars by the hundreds;
cloned armies; cloned workers who neither organize nor become
ill; cloning clinics with photos of "Your Next Baby," each a clone,
each with a price tag.

But then there are more defensible uses, such as cloning to
achieve a pregnancy when no other means is possible, or cloning
to avoid a genetic problem that lies in mitochondrial DNA. As
these more defensible uses become known to the public, will
opinion shift from opposition to acceptance? Will the distaste that
first greeted the prospect of human cloning give way to support?
If cloning becomes familiar, will it become acceptable? Or is the
opposition grounded in deeply held convictions and values?

Of course, one reason to oppose human cloning now is simply
that it is not safe. This is the objection noted by the National
Bioethics Advisory Commission, in their report to President Clinton, released on June 7, 1997 (see Appendix I, page 131). The
success rate will have to get substantially better than 1 in 277 (the
rate in the work that led up to the birth of Dolly) before anyone
would support using this technique to produce human beings.
But what then? What if safety improves to the point where there
is essentially no more risk for congenital anomaly or lost pregnancy than with natural means of conception? If cloning is safe,
will it be acceptable? Or is the opposition grounded in something
more abiding than worries about safety?

Christians, in particular, may wonder: Are there objections to
cloning that are grounded in theology? I want to explore some
theological concerns about cloning and offer a candid assessment

of how far they go in warning us to stay away from this technology. These concerns, I believe, offer important warnings about how cloning might be misused. At the same time, I do not believe that a compelling theological argument can be made against cloning for reproductive or for experimental purposes. But by probing the concerns that arise from our theology, as well as the worries of other people, by considering them carefully in public in the years and decades ahead, we improve our chances of preventing misuse of these new techniques.

Cloned Pre-Embryos and the Beginning of Life

As a result of the work at the Roslin Institute, it may soon become possible to use nuclear transfer cloning methods to produce human pre-embryos. If this were permitted, it would likely be quite beneficial to research. We would probably learn a great deal about how human genes regulate the complex processes by which a fertilized egg becomes an embryo, with its cells differentiating along various lines to become the many tissues and organs of the body. Such knowledge would very likely contribute to advances in medicine, especially in our ability to reverse cell differentiation and to be able to treat injuries and degenerative diseases.

Should we pursue this research? Many, of course, fervently believe that all human pre-embryo research is immoral and should be banned. It does not matter to them whether the pre-embryo is produced by cloning or by other means. All human pre-embryo experimentation is inherently immoral. They base this opposition on the theological belief that the full dignity of human personhood is present at or shortly after conception, and that we must not treat any human pre-embryo as an object of experimentation, no matter how lofty the research goal. To do so is to violate the pre-embryo's dignity as a human subject by engaging in research for which consent can never be given.

Others (myself included) hold a different view of the theological and moral status of the human pre-embryo.[2] It has a potential for personhood and thus should be accorded respect, but such respect is not inconsistent with every form of research. I am therefore prepared to argue that some forms of human pre-embryo research may be permitted, if these provisions are met: (1) the research protocols indicate that the pre-embryos are being accorded moral respect; (2) the pre-embryos are not allowed to develop beyond the 14-day stage; (3) they are not implanted; and (4) a compelling rationale can be offered for the research, either in terms of advances in fundamental knowledge or in the development of new medical procedures.

But now we have to face a new question: Does it matter if the pre-embryo is brought into existence by cloning? If we begin with the assumption that a human pre-embryo may be used in research, is it permissible to use a cloned human pre-embryo? And more precisely still: Does it matter if the cloned pre-embryo is created by division of another pre-embryo or if it is made, like Dolly, from a cell of an adult human person?

These are very difficult questions that require careful consideration before anyone should presume to engage in cloned human pre-embryo research. I am therefore somewhat alarmed that the recommendation of the National Bioethics Advisory Commission is that research with cloned pre-embryos not receive federal funds, but that it be permitted with private funds. This recommendation will likely mean that such research will proceed in private settings, far from the gaze of the public or the deliberations of ethicists.

If that is true, I would oppose such research. For such research to proceed, it must, I believe, be open to the public. Indeed, before research is undertaken, there should be widespread public discussion, and research should begin only if there is general public support. We should not expect unanimous support, but at the least a majority should support the notion of human pre-embryo research, cloned or otherwise, before research begins.

I think it is in the prudential interests of scientists and laboratories, private or public, that such discussion occur. Public support for science or technology can erode quickly, as in the case of support for nuclear power. It would be very sad indeed if public sentiment turned strongly against all genetics research because public opinion was not respected on the question of pre-embryo research. Scientists and laboratories should err on the side of caution in cultivating broad public understanding and support for these efforts.

The simple fact is that, as of 1997, we in the United States have not had anything resembling a public discussion of human pre-embryo research, nor have we even thought about how our views should be shaped by the opinions of people in other nations. Not just human cloning, but human germ-line experimentation[3] and pre-implantation screening[4] deserve public attention. There are many of us in the religious communities who would be prepared to argue for the appropriateness of responsible research in these areas, involving the experimental use of human pre-embryos, including cloning. But in the absence of public discussion, such research is wrong. Not only is it imprudent politically for scientists and laboratories to proceed without support; it is a violation of our collective right to consent to research that affects all human beings. And this consent—fully informed and carefully considered—is necessary before proceeding.

Identity, Individuality, and the Human Soul

Beyond the question of using cloning to produce pre-embryos for research lies the far broader question of producing a child by cloning. Some among us worry that, if someone were cloned, the original and the clone would be too much alike and one would violate the uniqueness or the individuality of the other. In the most extreme terms, some might think that the original and the clone are one person or share one soul, especially if they live at different times.

To what extent would we expect that an original and a clone would be alike? Would their likeness pose problems for either of them, and should cloning be opposed out of concern for these problems? Probably our best window into knowing how similar clones would be comes from our knowledge of "identical" or monozygotic (MZG) twins. Fortunately, twins have been studied extensively, and much is now known about their similarities and their differences.[5] As a result of these studies, scientists now have a pretty clear idea how much the similarities between MZG twins is due to their sharing the same genes and how much is due to their environment. For instance, most studies find that MZG twins are surprisingly alike, not just in appearance but in personality and in mental abilities, and that these similarities within pairs (and differences between pairs) are largely accounted for by genes.

Environment, of course, also plays a major role. In fact, studies of twins help to show just how important the role of environment actually is. The emerging picture is something like this: For most traits that we can measure, genes define or determine a range of possibilities, but the precise details are filled in over our lifetime as our genes interact with the environment. MZG twins, who share the same genes, inherit the same range of possibilities for many traits. Not surprisingly, they are similar in many ways. But they are also different; they are each unique individuals, with unique traits and unique personalities.

Many geneticists worry that nongeneticists tend to overestimate the power of genes to determine exactly who and what we are. They call this "genetic determinism" and fear that people all too readily use their genes as an excuse for behavior or as an explanation for everything about them. We should not overestimate the power of genes to determine the details of personality or behavior.

At the same time, we should not underestimate the significance of genes. MZG twins really are quite similar, notably more so than fraternal twins, a fact born out in a major study published in June 1997, involving 110 identical twin pairs and 130 same-sex fraternal pairs, all of whom were over eighty years old. Researchers found that, contrary to what we might expect, the influence of genes appears to increase rather than decrease over the course of the life span. Even so, environment remains important. "Although genetic influence on cognitive functioning late in life appears to be substantial, these data also demonstrate considerable environmental influence."[6]

In light of studies such as this, we need to acknowledge the significance of genetics in defining the limits of what is possible for us during our lifetime. But our genes only define a range of possibilities; they do not determine exactly what we will be. So we should never say that, because two individuals share the same genes, they are the same person or that they share the same soul.

The word "soul," which has staged something of a comeback in recent years, has arisen in the cloning discussion. In a recent essay in *Time* entitled "Can Souls Be Xeroxed?" the writer suggests that this question "assumes that psyches [or souls] get copied along with genes. That seems to be the prevailing assumption. . . . But many then proceed to talk excitedly about cloning as if it amounts to Xeroxing your soul."[7]

Just what does the word "soul" mean? The word has many meanings, even in recent Protestant theology. Some think of the soul as a special entity that lives in the body but is completely different from the body. If the body dies, the soul does not die but leaves the body. In this view, each clone could have its own soul—although it is possible to think that, if someone dies, his or her soul could come back in the clone. Someone wanting to clone a dead child in order to bring him or her back again may be thinking of the soul in this way.

Others think of the soul as the human relationship with God. The soul exists within us because God forms a covenant with us, conferring great value and dignity upon us, regardless of our capacities or our situation in life. For this view, every human being, cloned or otherwise, is valued by God as a unique covenant partner, and therefore has a unique soul.[8]

I see the human soul as a set of capacities. In a recent essay I offered this definition:

> According to Christian theology, human beings are like other animals in that we are made of the dust of the ground. But we are unlike all other animals in several important ways. Our mental capacities are far greater, our emotional sensitivities far more subtle, and our social relationships are more complex and rich than those of any other species. We alone have the capacity for language, for moral awareness, for free moral choice, for art, and, perhaps most important, for a relationship with God, a relationship which we believe will continue forever. These special capacities, taken together, are the human soul.[9]

In this view, each human soul—each specific set of capacities—is defined by genes but never entirely determined by them. Genes matter, but not by themselves. So even if we were to clone the genes, we could not copy the environment or the person's responses to the environment, so we could not copy the soul. Indeed, we must say that, while we can clone or copy the genes, we cannot clone or copy the organism, even the simplest organism. Every organism is a complex and nonrepeatable system of interactions between genes and environment. Every organism, and certainly every human person, cloned or not, is unique.

This view, which can be argued on the basis of genetics, is consistent with the Christian hope of the resurrection, which sees each human life as a unique, nonrepeatable journey through this mode of existence and into another that is more glorious and joyful. God does not send our souls back for another try. Any efforts to use cloning to "try to bring someone back" would be scientifically and theologically misguided.

Does any of this lead us to think that cloning is a bad idea? Yes, I think so. For by cloning a person, we would be recognizing something in that person that we want to copy, and we would try to achieve this by copying the genes. Precisely because genes do play a role in defining who we are, and even more because most people overestimate the power of genes to determine who we are, we should worry that the clone will be overwhelmed with a burden of living up to what we hope we are copying.

For example, if we clone a great athlete, we would hope that we would copy not merely the genes but the athletic ability. The clone, knowing our wishes, would find this burden of our expectations to be an insurmountable obstacle standing in the way of what is already difficult under any circumstances, namely, to define one's own identity. To bring a clone into existence, therefore, would be to subject a young person to an unacceptable burden of expectations.

This worry does not apply to every cloning scenario. For example, someone might want to clone a child who died in infancy, without having any idea of what the child might have become. The child's clone would then be largely free to define his or her own identity.

So I do not think that this worry should be seen as a categorical objection to cloning. Nonetheless, I do think that, if human cloning were allowed at all, it would soon be used to produce clones of people whose traits or abilities are known and admired, and I would worry very much about a child coming into existence with such a burden.

Is there a Natural Order of Procreation?

Since the Enlightenment, many in the West have thought of nature as a simple mass of raw materials upon which we human beings may impose our will, rearranging nature and now, with genetic engineering, re-designing it to suit our needs. We are beginning to see that this is misguided. In the name of bringing order to nature, we have destroyed complex ecosystems and threatened even our own survival.

So now many are asking whether nature has its own moral order that must be respected. Anyone who poses this question, however, recognizes that, if "bringing order to nature" has led to many evils, "imitating the order of nature" has produced even more. If nature is a competitive struggle for survival (as suggested in some interpretations of Darwin), then we should imitate its competitiveness. Because of such thinking, it has been argued that ethics consists precisely in not imitating nature.

Nevertheless, it is right to ask whether there are regularities and orders in nature that deserve our respect, that we violate at our own peril, and that we transgress only because we delude ourselves into thinking we are not part of nature, but stand aloof from it like some sort of technological gods. Recently, several theologians have suggested that we need to recognize that nature's order deserves our respect. In part, such a view is grounded on Genesis 1, in which God declares creation good before human beings arrive on the scene. That is, creation is good in its own order and in its relationship to God. Human beings, coming into nature (or as we would now say, arising from it), must respect the ordered value of that which is already here.

Langdon Gilkey, for example, has recently argued that the separating of value from nature is both dangerous and false: "My entire argument has contested this radical sundering of nature and value, of blind objective process and subjective purposing or valuing."[10] Further, "The sharp modern or secular split between objective nature and subjective values makes intelligible neither science nor the humanities, neither nature nor humanism, neither technology nor democracy."[11]

How might we apply this to human cloning? Is there an order of nature that would be violated by bringing a person into existence by cloning? The argument might run like this: The earliest organisms produced asexually, essentially by cloning. A momentous evolutionary advance occurred with sexual reproduction, allowing the reshuffling of genes in every generation and permitting far more genetic diversity to appear. Evolution could then occur more quickly and go in many directions, including our own. Furthermore, as creatures became more complex and needed parents to rear them, sexual reproduction assured that both parents have a genetic interest in their offspring, so sexual reproduction can be seen as ultimately encouraging the care of offspring by two parents. For human beings, this parental investment must be substantial if the child is to thrive. Sexual reproduction creates a genetic bond between both parents and the child. At the same time, the child is unique—that is, a combination of both parents but a copy of neither. Cloning, by returning us to asexual reproduction, would violate this natural order that is so beneficial to the child. Other reproductive techniques, such as in vitro fertilization, if the sperm and egg come from the couple, respect the order of nature in that the child is a unique combination of the parents' genes.

Does this argument provide a compelling reason for opposing human cloning? For many people, yes. And for others who may not find it compelling, it will point nonetheless to something that is intuitively attractive, namely, that children should come into the world with every advantage possible. Having two genetic parents while being different from each would seem to be an advantage.

While I am sympathetic with the argument and do in fact believe that it points to an important benefit for children that could be lost by cloning, I do not find the argument entirely persuasive. This argument for a "natural order of the family" has been misused, I believe, to support all too narrow views of families and to discriminate against those who, for whatever reason, find themselves in family relationships that do not wholly conform to the order. We should be profoundly suspicious of an argument that has been used in so many destructive ways.

But suppose we could prevent any misuse of the argument. Does it then make a valid point against cloning? Only if we think we have learned how to read values off nature (much like reading the temperature off a thermometer) rather than merely project our values into nature. In my own Reformed tradition, we have learned to be deeply suspicious of ourselves in this regard. All too readily in the past, we human beings have used our ideas about natural order to justify racism, unchecked competitiveness, genocide, and war. And so while the argument that cloning violates the order of nature seems to point to something very serious and important, I do not find it persuasive because I cannot trust that we know how to find moral guidance in nature.

As the Reformed tradition affirms, Christians find their best clue about nature by looking at Jesus Christ, where we see nature rightly related to God and where we see its destiny prefigured in Christ's resurrection. In Jesus Christ, we see a welcoming of children that transcends genetic parentage. From this we might infer that cloning is a matter of indifference. It may not be something Christians will choose (they might prefer adoption), but it is not something they will try to prohibit.

While I find this particular argument (that cloning violates natural order) to be less than compelling, it seems to me that this is a subject that needs much more attention. Different Christian traditions have taken decidedly different stances here, with Roman Catholicism arguing strongly that there is a moral order of nature that would be violated by cloning while some Protestants neglect nature almost entirely. We need to understand each other more fully here. In particular, we need to understand what it means to believe in a God who creates all things, ordering them toward their destiny in Christ.

Our ignorance is vast, our understanding limited, and our discussion has only begun. We stand, as it were, at Day One of the new century, at the beginning of a new era. For now, the weight of theological conviction is against the use of cloning to produce a child. It will be up to those who want to pursue cloning to make the stronger argument.

NOTES

1. For example, a poll reported in *Time* indicates that 91% would not clone themselves and 74% believe it is against God's will to clone human beings; *Time*, March 10, 1997, 71.

2. For a discussion, see Ronald Cole-Turner and Brent Waters, *Pastoral Genetics: Theology and Care at the Beginning of Life* (Cleveland: Pilgrim Press, 1996).

3. Germ-line genetic alteration would alter all cells in the human body, including sex cells, and thus would be transmitted to future generations. This is usually distinguished from somatic cell gene therapy, which only alters the cells of affected tissues. It is reassuring that a major biotechnology industry group has adopted this position regarding germ-line and cloning research: "We will not. . . treat genetic disorders by altering the genes of human sperm or eggs until the medical, ethical and social issues that will arise from this kind of therapy have been more broadly discussed and clarified. Also, we support continuation of the voluntary moratorium on the potential cloning of entire human beings." The Biotechnology Industry Organization, "Statement of Principles," (Washington, D.C.: August 1997), 3.

4. First reported in Alan H. Handyside et al., "Birth of a Normal Girl after In Vitro Fertilization and Preimplantation Diagnostic Testing for Cystic Fibrosis," *The New England Journal of Medicine* 327 (1992): 905–10.

5. For example, see Thomas J. Bouchard, Jr., et al., "Sources of Human Psychological Differences: The Minnesota Study of Twins Reared Apart," *Science* 250 (1990): 223–28; and Robert Plomin, Michael J. Owen, and Peter McGuffin, "The Genetic Basis Complex Human Behaviors," *Science* 264 (1994): 1733–39.

6. Gerald E. McClearn, et al., "Substantial Genetic Influence on Cognitive Abilities in Twins 80 or More Years Old," *Science* 275 (1997): 1560–63, at 1563.

7. Robert Wright, "Can Souls Be Xeroxed?," *Time* , March 10, 1997, 73.

8. This view is suggested by Ted Peters on p. 19.

9. Ronald Cole-Turner, "Human Nature as Seen by Science and Faith," *In Whose Image: Theology, Biology, and Human Nature* (Louisville, Ky., 1997, forthcoming).

10. Langdon Gilkey, *Nature, Reality, and the Sacred: The Nexus of Science and Religion* (Minneapolis: Fortress Press, 1993), 111.

11. Ibid., 112.

Appendix I:
Recommendations of the National
Bioethics Advisory Commission

Chapter 6 of Cloning Human Beings,
Report and Recommendations of the National
Bioethics Advisory Commission,
June 9, 1997, Rockville, Md., 107-110

With the announcement that an apparently quite normal sheep had been born in Scotland as a result of somatic cell nuclear transfer cloning came the realization that, as a society, we must yet again collectively decide whether and how to use what appeared to be a dramatic new technological power. The promise and the peril of this scientific advance was noted immediately around the world, but the prospects of creating human beings through this technique mainly elicited widespread resistance and/or concern. Despite this reaction, the scientific significance of the accomplishment, in terms of improved understanding of cell development and cell differentiation, should not be lost. The challenge to public policy is to support the myriad beneficial applications of this new technology, while simultaneously guarding against its more questionable uses.

Much of the negative reaction to the potential application of such cloning in humans can be attributed to fears about harms to the children who may result, particularly psychological harms associated with a possibly diminished sense of individuality and personal autonomy. Others express concern about a degradation in the quality of parenting and family life. And virtually all people agree that the current risks of physical harm to children associated with somatic cell nuclear transplantation cloning justify a prohibition at this time on such experimentation.

In addition to concerns about specific harms to children, people have frequently expressed fears that a widespread practice of somatic cell nuclear transfer cloning would undermine important social values by opening the door to a form of eugenics or by tempting some to manipulate others as if they were objects instead of persons. Arrayed against these concerns are other important social values, such as protecting personal choice, particularly in matters pertaining to procreation and child rearing, maintaining privacy and the freedom of scientific inquiry, and encouraging the possible development of new biomedical breakthroughs.

As somatic cell nuclear transfer cloning could represent a means of human reproduction for some people, limitations on that choice must be made only when the societal benefits of prohibition clearly outweigh the value of maintaining the private nature of such highly personal decisions. Especially in light of some arguably compelling cases for attempting to clone a human being using somatic cell nuclear transfer, the ethics of policy making must strike a balance between the values society wishes to reflect and issues of privacy and the freedom of individual choice.

To arrive at its recommendations concerning the use of somatic cell nuclear transfer techniques, NBAC also examined long-standing religious traditions that often influence and guide citizens' responses to new technologies. Religious positions on human cloning are pluralistic in their premises, modes of argument, and conclusions. Nevertheless, several major themes are prominent in Jewish, Roman Catholic, Protestant, and Islamic positions, including responsible human dominion over nature, human dignity and destiny, procreation, and family life. Some religious thinkers argue that the use of somatic cell nuclear transfer cloning to create a child would be intrinsically immoral and thus could never be morally justified; they usually propose a ban on such human cloning. Other religious thinkers contend that human cloning to create a child could be morally justified under some circumstances but hold that it should be strictly regulated in order to prevent abuses.

The public policies recommended with respect to the creation of a child using somatic cell nuclear transfer reflect the Commission's best judgments about both the ethics of attempting such an experiment and our view of traditions regarding limitations on individual actions in the name of the common good. At present, the use of this technique to create a child would be a premature experiment that exposes the developing child to unacceptable risks. This in itself is sufficient to justify a prohibition on cloning human beings at this time, even if such efforts were to be characterized as the exercise of a fundamental right to attempt to procreate. More speculative psychological harms to the child, and effects on the moral, religious, and cultural values of society, may be enough to justify continued prohibitions in the future, but more time is needed for discussion and evaluation of these concerns.

Beyond the issue of the safety of the procedure, however, NBAC found that concerns relating to the potential psychological harms to children and effects on the moral, religious, and cultural values of society merited further reflection and deliberation. Whether upon such further deliberation our nation will conclude that the use of cloning techniques to create children should be allowed or permanently banned is, for the moment, an open question. Time is an ally in this regard, allowing for the accrual of further data from animal experimentation, enabling an assessment of the prospective safety and efficacy of the procedure in humans, as well as granting a period of fuller national debate on ethical and social concerns. The Commission therefore concluded that there should be imposed a period of time in which no attempt is made to create a child using somatic cell nuclear transfer.

Within this overall framework the Commission came to the following conclusions and recommendations:

I. The Commission concludes that at this time it is morally unacceptable for anyone in the public or private sector, whether in a research or clinical setting, to attempt to create a child using somatic cell nuclear transfer cloning. We have reached a consensus on this point because current scientific information indicates that this technique is not safe to use in humans at this time. Indeed, we believe it would violate important ethical obligations were clinicians or researchers to attempt to create a child using these particular technologies, which are likely to involve unacceptable risks to the fetus and/or potential child. Moreover, in addition to safety concerns, many other serious ethical concerns have been identified, which require much more widespread and careful public deliberation before this technology may be used.

The Commission, therefore, recommends the following for immediate action:

A continuation of the current moratorium on the use of federal funding in support of any attempt to create a child by somatic cell nuclear transfer.

An immediate request to all firms, clinicians, investigators, and professional societies in the private and non-federally funded sectors to comply voluntarily with the intent of the federal moratorium. Professional and scientific societies should make clear that any attempt to create a child by somatic cell nuclear transfer and implantation into a woman's body would at this time be an irresponsible, unethical, and unprofessional act.

II. The Commission further recommends that:

Federal legislation should be enacted to prohibit anyone from attempting, whether in a research or clinical setting, to create a child through somatic cell nuclear transfer cloning. It is critical, however, that such legislation include a sunset clause to ensure that Congress will review the issue after a specified time period (three to five years) in order to decide whether the prohibition continues to be needed. If state legislation is enacted, it should also contain such a sunset provision. Any such legislation or associated regulation also ought to require that at some point prior to the expiration of the sunset period, an appropriate oversight body will evaluate and report on the current status of somatic cell nuclear transfer technology and on the ethical and social issues that its potential use to create human beings would raise in light of public understandings at that time.

III. The Commission also concludes that:

Any regulatory or legislative actions undertaken to effect the foregoing prohibition on creating a child by somatic cell nuclear transfer should be carefully written so as not to interfere with other important areas of scientific research. In particular, no new regulations are required regarding the cloning of human DNA sequences and cell lines, since neither activity raises the scientific and ethical issues that arise from the attempt to create children through somatic cell nuclear transfer, and these fields of research have already provided important scientific and biomedical advances. Likewise, research on cloning animals by somatic cell nuclear transfer does not raise the issues implicated in attempting to use this technique for human cloning, and its continuation should only be subject to existing regulations regarding the humane use of animals and review by institution-based animal protection committees.

If a legislative ban is not enacted, or if a legislative ban is ever lifted, clinical use of somatic cell nuclear transfer techniques to create a child should be preceded by research trials that are governed by the twin protections of independent review and informed consent, consistent with existing norms of human subjects protection.

The United States Government should cooperate with other nations and international organizations to enforce any common aspects of their respective policies on the cloning of human beings.

IV. The Commission also concludes that different ethical and religious perspectives and traditions are divided on many of the important moral issues that surround any attempt to create a child using somatic cell nuclear transfer techniques. Therefore, we recommend that:

The federal government, and all interested and concerned parties, encourage widespread and continuing deliberation on these issues in order to further our understanding of the ethical and social implications of this technology and to enable society to produce appropriate long-term policies regarding this technology should the time come when present concerns about safety have been addressed.

V. Finally, because scientific knowledge is essential for all citizens to participate in a full and informed fashion in the governance of our complex society, the Commission recommends that:

Federal departments and agencies concerned with science should cooperate in seeking out and supporting opportunities to provide information and education to the public in the area of genetics, and on other developments in the biomedical sciences, especially where these affect important cultural practices, values, and beliefs.

Appendix II:
Denominational
Statements on Cloning

Editor's note: These statements were available at the time this book went to press. Since then, other church bodies have also issued statements.

1. The General Assembly of the Church of Scotland,
   May 22, 1997, pp. 138

2. The Secretariat for Pro-Life Activities of the
   National Conference of Catholic Bishops,
   February 25, 1997, pp. 142

3. The United Methodist Genetic Science Task Force,
   May 9, 1997, pp. 143

4. The Christian Life Commission
   of the Southern Baptist Convention,
   March 6, 1997, pp. 146

5. The Genetics Committee of the United Church Board
   for Homeland Ministries of the United Church of Christ,
   June 9, 1997, pp. 147

"Motions on Cloning" Passed by the General Assembly of the Church of Scotland on 22 May 1997

1. Commend the principle of the production of proteins of therapeutic value in the milk of genetically modified sheep and other farm animals, but oppose, and urge Her Majesty's Government to take necessary steps to prevent, the application of animal cloning as a routine procedure in meat and milk production, as an unacceptable commodification of animals.

2. Reaffirm their belief in the basic dignity and uniqueness of each human being under God. Express the strongest possible opposition to the cloning of human beings and urge Her Majesty's Government to press for a comprehensive international treaty to ban it worldwide.

"Cloning Animals and Humans: A Supplementary Report to the 1997 General Assembly" from the Society, Religion and Technology Project, Board of National Mission

Introduction

In February 1997, Dolly the cloned sheep became a global news sensation. Scientists at the Roslin Institute and PPL Therapeutics outside Edinburgh had rewritten the laws of biology in producing a live sheep by cloning from cells of the udder of an adult ewe by nuclear transfer.

The Director of the Church of Scotland's Society, Religion and Technology Project quickly became a focus for ethical comment, with numerous TV, radio, newspaper and magazine interviews and articles, including BBC's *Newsnight* and *Heart of the Matter* programmes, and German and Dutch national television. These opportunities arose because the SRT Project was already involved in assessing the issue, having for the last three years had an expert working group on the ethical issues of genetic engineering, one of whose members is the Roslin scientist who "produced"

Dolly, Dr. Ian Wilmut. As a result, SRT was in a unique position to offer informed and balanced comment to the world's media, and to influence the course of a debate in which sensation and ill-judged speculation were rife.

A very significant development was the fact that quite a lot of media picked up SRT's involvement from the Internet. This was because Dr. Bruce had written an article on the ethics of cloning at the time of the first Roslin cloning discovery a year before, and had included this in SRT's own site on the World Wide Web. When the news broke, press agencies like CNN News searched for "cloning" on the Internet and found SRT's article as one of very few in existence. They put in a link to SRT from their own site, and all the world has since been following the trail—a month later, the SRT article was still receiving 400 Internet "visits" every day. This speaks volumes for the importance of SRT's work at the cutting edge of some of the most important issues which science is raising for our times. SRT identified four main issues—the basic genetic engineering work at Roslin, whether we should already clone animals, whether we might one day clone humans, and how such research should be controlled and kept accountable to the public.

Cloning Animals

Much of the media attention focused on speculation about cloning humans, but missed the more immediate impact on animals, and the ethical questions on how far we should apply technology to them. The cloning arose from Roslin's search for more effective ways to do the existing work at PPL Therapeutics of genetically engineering sheep to produce therapeutic proteins in sheep's and cow's milk. The first product for emphysema and cystic fibrosis sufferers is undergoing clinical trials, and a range of other medical applications is in prospect. The SRT Project working group had already found this work generally ethically acceptable. There were clear human benefits, with few animal welfare or other concerns once past the experimental stage.

The new method should enable Roslin to do a more precise genetic modification using less experimental animals, but the side effect is that the resulting sheep is a clone, genetically almost identical to its founder. PPL might clone 5–10 sheep from a single genetically modified animal, but would then breed naturally thereafter to give flocks of varied sheep, but all containing the desired genetic modification. On this very limited scale, this would not seem ethically unacceptable. The possibility that farm animals might be cloned routinely for meat or milk production on a large scale is however a very different matter. In animal breeding, the need to maintain genetic diversity sets practical limits on how far cloning would make sense, but certain applications are already being considered. A breeder might wish to clone the best breeding stock to sell for feeding up for slaughter, or to found new nucleus herds. Would this be carrying our use of animals one stage too far?

For the Christian, the world around us is God's creation. Variety is one of its characteristic features, and especially at the level of higher animals and humans. The overall picture in the Bible, in commandments, stories and poetry, is of a creation whose sheer diversity is itself a cause of praise to its creator. To reduce this diversity to a strict blueprint, and produce replica animals routinely on demand, would seem to go against something basic and God-given about the nature of life. The very fact that selective breeding has its limits reflects this fact. Some would argue that cloning is thus absolutely wrong, no matter what it was being used for. SRT argues that scale and intention play a part. PPL's limited context could be acceptable since the main intention was not the clone as such but growing an animal of a known genetic composition, where natural methods would not work. What would be unacceptable would be in routine animal production, where natural methods exist, but would be side-stepped on the grounds of economics or convenience. This would represent one step too far beyond conventional selective breeding in the way we use animals as commodities. The approach that, whatever use we find for animals, we could clone them to do it more efficiently brings the mass production principles of the factory too far into the animal kingdom. Just as in the Old Testament an ox was not to be muzzled while treading out the grain, animals have certain freedoms which we should preserve. We may use animals to an extent, but we need to remind ourselves that they are firstly God's creatures, to whom we may not do everything we like.

Human Cloning

One of the abiding SciFi nightmares has been the idea that we could one day replicate human beings asexually, just by copying material from human cells. Roslin's scientists told a Select Committee of the House of Commons that the nuclear transfer technique they have applied to produce Dolly could be in theory applied to humans, but the headlines which ran "human cloning in two years" were irresponsible exaggerations. It is by no means a foregone conclusion. Dr. Wilmut and his colleagues made it quite clear that they think that to clone humans would be unethical, and most people seem to agree.

The Church of Scotland has already stated that to clone human beings would be ethically unacceptable as a matter of principle. On principle, to replicate any human technologically is a violation of the basic dignity and uniqueness of each human being made in God's image, of what God has given to that individual and to no one else. It is not the same as twinning. There is a world of difference ethically between choosing to clone from a known existing individual and the unpredictable occurrence of twins of unknown nature in the womb. The nature of cloning is that of an instrumental use of both the clone and the one cloned as means to an end, for someone else's benefit. This represents unacceptable human abuse, and a potential for exploitation which should be outlawed worldwide.

In 1990 the UK pioneered legislation making human cloning research illegal, but currently it would be allowed in the USA and several EU countries, and many other cultures with very different value systems. Some form of international treaty should be called for whereby no country would allow cloning research to be carried over from animals to humans. Realistically, there would be no way to stop a back street clinic or a dictatorship from ignoring such a treaty, but the lines need to be drawn. A second line of defense is also called for—the notion of the ethical scientist, for whom it would be against all professional principles to pursue such research. Some have argued that research should be permitted into the possibility of cloning living transplant organs from body cells. This would require more careful ethical consideration, but the danger of a "slippery slope" to full human cloning would loom large over such an enterprise.

This raises a last question of the control of such research. In many spheres of research there is a deficit in public accountability in the existing procedures whereby research priorities are set. There are no easy solutions to this problem, but, at the very least, it points to the need for a standing ethical commission on non-human biotechnology, whose work is open to public comment and scrutiny, in which those areas of research which are especially likely to have far-reaching ethical implications are first debated in public.

"Remarks in Response to News Reports on the Cloning of Mammals," by the Secretariat for Pro-Life Activities of the National Conference of Catholic Bishops, February 25, 1997

Recent reports about successful cloning in mammals have rightly raised ethical concerns about human cloning. Catholic teaching rejects the cloning of human beings, because this is not a worthy way to bring a human being into the world. Children have a right to have real parents, and to be conceived as the fruit of marital love between husband and wife. They are not products we can manufacture to our specifications. Least of all should they be produced as deliberate "copies" of other people to ensure that they have certain desired features.

Donum Vitae, issued in 1987 by the Holy See's Congregation for the Doctrine of the Faith, reminded us that human life is a "gift of inestimable value" over which we must exercise careful stewardship. "The one conceived must be the fruit of parents' love," not treated as the product of a laboratory technique. Efforts to clone human embryos are also unethical because they would subject developing members of the human family, who cannot give informed consent, to risky experiments that cannot benefit them as individuals.

Such technologies should prompt us once again to appreciate a basic truth: The fact that it is technically possible to do something doesn't mean it ought to be done.

Richard M. Doerflinger
Secretariat for Pro-Life Activities
National Conference of Catholic Bishops

February 25, 1997

"Statement from the United Methodist
Genetic Science Task Force,"
May 9, 1997

(This is a statement by the Genetic Science Task Force of the United Methodist Church. Only the General Conference speaks for the entire church. The Task Force was commissioned by the United Methodist General Board of Church and Society.)

Cloning has sparked enormous and sustained concern in the general public, including the church. It touches on many crucial questions about human nature, raises hopes and expectations, and brings to the fore uncertainties and fears. These include fears with substantial social and theological ramifications—fears that people will be used or abused, that women will be exploited, that the fabric of the family will be torn, that human distinctiveness will be compromised, fears that genetic diversity will be lessened, that corporate profit and personal gain will control the direction of research and development, and that privacy will be invaded. While we do not see obvious benefits of human cloning and recognize potential dangers of animal and tissue cloning, we also acknowledge the excitement that this new research generates for advances in medicine, agriculture, and other scientific endeavors.

As United Methodists, our reflections on these issues emerge from our faith. When we think about cloning, we remember that creation has its origin, value, and destiny in God, that humans are stewards of creation, and that technology has brought both great benefit and harm to creation. As people of faith, we believe that our identity as humans is more than our genetic inheritance, our social environment, or the sum of the two. We are created by God and have been redeemed by Jesus Christ. In light of these theological claims and other questions, fears, and expectations, we recognize that our present human knowledge on this issue is incomplete and finite. We do not know all the consequences of cloning (psychological, social, or genetic). It is important that the limits of human knowledge be considered as policy is made.

1. At this time, we call for a ban on human cloning. This would include all intended projects, privately or governmentally funded, to advance human cloning. (For the purposes of this document, human

cloning means the intentional production of identical humans and human embryos.)

2. We call for a ban on therapeutic, medical, and research procedures which generate waste embryos.

3. As Christians, we affirm that all human beings, regardless of the method of reproduction, are children of God and bear the Image of God. If humans were ever cloned, they along with all other human beings, would have inherent value, dignity, and moral status and should have the same civil rights (in keeping with principles found in the United Nations Declaration of Human Rights). There must be no discrimination against any person because of reproductive origins. The same principles of autonomy, consent and equality of opportunity would apply as fully to cloned human beings as to any other.

4. If research on human cloning does proceed, we urge that the impact on affected populations be given particular consideration—especially those whose voices often go unheard. These would include the women whose health and well-being might be affected, their offspring, the families, infertile men and women, and those who would be denied access to these technologies. We urge consideration of the psychological and social effects on individuals, families, parental relationships, and the larger society. Those presently affected by in vitro fertilization, surrogacy, artificial insemination, and other reproductive technologies should be consulted to provide insights into some related psychological and social issues.

5. We urge the widespread discussion of issues related to cloning in public forums including churches. Given the profound theological and moral implications, the imperfection of human knowledge, and the tremendous potential risks and benefits, we urge that any moves toward cloning proceed slowly until these issues can be discussed fully both by the general public as well as by experts in agricultural and biological science, social science, public policy, ethics, theology, law, and medicine, including genetics and genetic counseling. In addition, discussion and policy making must include input from communities of faith.

6. Acknowledging that market forces play a significant role in the development of new technologies, we want appropriate social and governmental bodies to guide and monitor research and development in this field. Concern for profit and commercial advantage should be balanced

by consideration for individual rights, the valid interest of wide con-
stituencies, and the common good, including the good of future generations.

Questions to Be Addressed

Many questions must be addressed in a discussion of cloning, including the following:

Is there a compelling argument for human cloning? Are there enough
clear benefits to outweigh the risks?

Is human cloning the only or best way to arrive at these benefits?

Is human cloning in the best interest of those affected—particularly
children, women, families, and parents?

How do we exercise stewardship in the allocation of scarce resources? Would money and human effort be better spent on other forms
of research?

How can societies effectively implement, enforce, and maintain
cloning guidelines and regulations nationally and globally? What measures can be taken to discourage the misuse of these technologies and the
exploitation of human beings?

"Resolution on Cloning" adopted by the Trustees of the Christian Life Commission of the Southern Baptist Convention, March 6, 1997

Whereas, on February 27, 1997, Ian Wilmut and colleagues in Scotland announced the first successful cloning of a mammalian species, and

Whereas researchers in Oregon announced March 1, 1997, the successful cloning of a rhesus monkey, and

Whereas on March 4, 1997, President Clinton announced a prohibition on federal funding for human cloning research, and

Whereas Southern Baptists are on record for their strong affirmation of the sanctity and uniqueness of every human life;

Be it therefore resolved that we, the trustees of the Southern Baptist Convention's Christian Life Commission, meeting on March 6, 1997, do affirm the President's decision to prohibit federal funding for human cloning research, and

Be it further resolved that we request that the Congress of the United States make human cloning unlawful, and

Be it further resolved that we call for all nations of the world to make efforts to prevent the cloning of any human being.

"Statement on Cloning" by the
United Church of Christ Committee on Genetics

The following is a statement of the United Church of Christ Committee on Genetics and is not an official statement of the United Church of Christ. The Committee on Genetics was appointed by the United Church Board for Homeland Ministries, in cooperation with the United Church Board for World Ministries, the Office for Church in Society, and the Council for Health and Human Service Ministries. The Committee will submit this statement for consideration as a resolution at the 21st General Synod of the United Church of Christ, meeting in Columbus, Ohio, July 3–8, 1997.

The announcement in February of the birth of Dolly the cloned sheep raises important ethical and religious questions. We who serve on the United Church of Christ Committee on Genetics are grateful for the careful and dedicated work of scientists such as Ian Wilmot and for the ways in which their discoveries can improve human health. We acknowledge that scientists themselves have been among the first to call for restraint in this field of research. We also applaud the request by President Clinton that the National Bioethics Advisory Commission (NBAC) prepare a report on the ethics of cloning, and that the NBAC eagerly sought the opinions of religious leaders in preparing its report. Because we believe that all new technologies should be developed with due regard for morality and social justice, we urge the continuation of the Bioethics Commission as a national forum for discussion of the ethics of emerging fields of research, including human cloning and germ-line experimentation.

1. Regarding the Use of Cloning
to Produce a Human Person

The United Church of Christ is fundamentally committed to justice. We experience a tension with regard to cloning, therefore. On the one hand, we are aware that our culture has allowed, even encouraged, the development of many technologies geared to permit couples to have children "of their own"—meaning children who are genetically related to them. Cloning might allow some couples to have children whose genes come from that couple and are not an admixture with genes from "outside" the committed relationship. Thus, on the one hand, justice seems to press for allowing the same privileges (some would say rights) for those couples as are currently allowed for others.

At the same time, a concern for justice raises questions about the validity of all new reproductive technologies—artificial insemination, in vitro fertilization, etc. When the world groans with hunger, when children are stunted from chronic malnutrition, when people die of famine by the thousands every day—when this is the reality of the world in which we live, the development of any more technologies to suit the desires of those who are relatively privileged, secure, and comfortable seems to fly in the face of fundamental claims of justice.

For this reason, in spite of our empathy with couples who might seek cloning in order to have children "of their own," we oppose cloning and say "enough" to technologies that are privileges of the rich in the Western world. We support legislation to ban cloning for reproductive purposes, at least for the foreseeable future.

At the same time, should someone produce a cloned child, we would insist absolutely that such a child is a full human being, created in the image of God and entitled to all human and civil rights. This conviction is grounded both in our theological belief in the uniqueness of each person as a child of God and in the insights of genetics, which show us that genes and environment interact at every stage to produce the phenotype or the organism. Accordingly, we believe that while genes can be cloned or copied, the phenotype or the person cannot be cloned or copied but is always a unique expression of the interplay between genes and environment. We recognize that there is widespread confusion among the general public about the role of genes in determining who we are as persons. In this respect, genetic science and Christian faith agree in criticizing what is sometimes called "genetic determinism." We hope the United Church of Christ will play a helpful role in educating the public about the important but quite limited role of genes in determining the full meaning of human identity and personhood.

In addition to these fundamental concerns regarding justice and respect for all created life, members of the committee raised the following concerns:

First, there is evidence that the current state of technique of nuclear transfer cloning is far too imprecise to meet minimal expectations of safety that should be met before they are applied to human beings. Whether the safety level can be improved sufficiently through research with other mammals will remain to be seen. It is possible the future research will remove this concern. Our second and third reasons, however, are moral in nature and are not likely to be affected by the future level of technical ability.

Second, it is possible that a child produced by cloning would suffer from an overwhelming burden of expectations. Anyone wanting to create such a child would have a prior knowledge of what this child's genes could become and would in part make the decision to clone on the basis of that knowledge. That prior knowledge would create a weight of expectation against which such a child would have to define his or her own identity. Precisely because "genetic determinism" is so widespread in contemporary culture, this weight of expectation would likely be inconsistent with the freedom necessary for each person to develop an individual identity.

Third, many observers believe that it is beneficial for children to have the genetic resources of two adults that are recombined to form a genotype that is unique and yet tied genetically to both adults. This assures that, in terms of nuclear DNA, the child is related to both adults yet different from either. If children were produced by nuclear transfer cloning, their nuclear DNA would not have this relatedness and this difference.

2. Regarding the Use of Cloning
to Produce Human Pre-Embryos for Research

Nuclear transfer cloning might also be used to produce human preembryos for research purposes through the 14th day of embryonic development. It is very likely that through such means, scientists could learn a great deal about basic human developmental biology and that this knowledge might someday lead to treatments for degenerative conditions or to counteract some forms of sterility. Whether such research is permissible ultimately raises the question of the theological and moral status of the human pre-embryo. Beginning with the 8th General Synod

in 1971, various General Synods of the United Church of Christ have regarded the human pre-embryo as due great respect, consistent with its
potential to develop into full human personhood. General Synods have
not, however, regarded the pre-embryo as the equivalent of a person.

Therefore, we on the United Church of Christ Committee on Genetics do not object categorically to human pre-embryo research, including
research that produces and studies cloned human pre-embryos through
the 14th day of fetal development, provided the research is well justified in terms of its objectives, that the research protocols show proper
respect for the pre-embryos, and that they not be implanted. We urge
public discussion of current research and future possibilities, ranging
from pre-implantation genetic screening of human pre-embryos to nuclear transfer cloning to human germ-line experimentation. We do not
categorically oppose any of these areas of research, but we believe they
must be pursued, if at all, within the framework of broad public discussion. In 1989, the 17th General Synod of the United Church of Christ
stated that it was "cautious at present about procedures that would
make genetic changes which humans would transmit to their offspring
(germline therapy). . . . We urge extensive public discussion and, as
appropriate, the development of federal guidelines during the period
when germline therapy becomes feasible." We would urge legislation to
ensure that all research on human pre-embryos, even that which is privately funded, would be reviewed by Institutional Review Boards in
accordance with federal regulations.

Now with the possibility of human cloning by nuclear transfer, this
call for public discussion becomes all the more urgent. Current US federal law prohibits the use of federal funding for all pre-embryo research.
Such research occurs in other countries and in the United States, funded
by private sources. As a result, human pre-embryo research proceeds
legally in the US, but there is little or no public discussion of its ethics.

We on the United Church of Christ Committee on Genetics are opposed to the idea that human pre-embryo research, such as human germ-
line experimentation or research involving cloned pre-embryos, should
be permitted but left largely unregulated if funded privately, or that there
is no federal responsibility for the ethics of such research if federal funds
are not used. We believe that this approach merely seeks to avoid the
difficult public deliberation that should occur prior to such research. We

believe that all such research should be subject to broad public comment and that it should only proceed within a context of public understanding and general public support.

3. Regarding Cloning
of Non-Human Mammalian Species

We on the United Church of Christ Committee on Genetics believe that the use of nuclear transfer cloning in research on non-human mammalian species is morally and theologically permissible, provided, of course, that animals be treated humanely and that needless suffering is avoided. Nevertheless, we are concerned that the use of nuclear transfer cloning, together with other genetic and reproductive technologies, will contribute to a diminished regard for non-human species. In particular, we lament the attitude that non-human species have no inherent dignity or significance beyond their usefulness to human beings. We confess with regret that in the past, the Christian church itself has often encouraged such a utilitarian view of non-human species. In contrast to our own past, the General Synod of the United Church of Christ stated in 1989 that "God is Creator of all and confers value upon all creatures. . . . Therefore, we respect each creature as valuable to God beyond its apparent usefulness to us." Such an attitude of respect does not entirely preclude our use of animals in research or for other purposes. But we are concerned that cloning, together with other technologies, might contribute to the view that non-human animals, particularly mammals, are little more than pharmaceutical factories, or convenient sources of donor organs for human patients, or valuable research tools. While we do not object specifically to any of these uses of mammalian nuclear transfer cloning, we are concerned nonetheless that these uses will contribute to a disregard for the dignity that all non-human species enjoy by virtue of their relation to God the Creator. Further, because of the danger of narrowing genetic diversity (and thus of diminishing the God-given complexity of creation) we do not think that animal cloning should ever be widely used, for instance in agricultural application.